Patti Boyle has extensive experience in career coaching, organizational consulting and entrepreneurship. In this book, she combines that professional experience with her life experience to provide the kind of in-depth career advice that is usually offered for hundreds of dollars an hour. Readers with a serious interest in career development will surely find useful ideas and suggestions in this book.

—Orville Pierson, Author of *The Unwritten Rules of the Highly Effective Job Search*

This book captures the passion and the possibility of what all life has to offer so you can fulfill your destiny. TAKE THIS JOB and LOVE IT! is a guide to help you create your vision and find your purpose to live your ideal life. It is a must read for any person at any age.

—Kim Nugent, Ed. D., Author Promotion *Protocol, Unlock the Secrets of Promotability & Career Success, Coaching Conversations, Paving Your Path, What's Next for High School Graduates.*

Patti Boyle's book provides positive, helpful advice for job seekers, while relating her own inspiring journey. Her insights on the intangible and internalized aspects so often overlooked but critical to job search success are right on point. She also wisely reminds us how important it is to have compassion for all who are involved in job loss, whether it's the employee being let go during a layoff or the employee who remains and experiences survivor guilt. Outstanding!

—Angela Loeb, author of
What You Need To Know To Get A Job Now!,
Job Search Tactics That Work, and
The Day You Find Out Why

TAKE THIS JOB and LOVE IT! is an inspirational, thought-provoking, and heartfelt guide that will support you in discovering the gift and calling you were created to share with the world.

—Dawn Mitchell Owens
Author of *Light After a Layoff*

Patti's powerful and intimate story that led to her unique calling in life makes this book a compelling read. Through her personal and professional challenges in transitioning from a career in education, she allows us to share her

C-Suite successes, entrepreneurial accomplishments and her extensive experience doing what she absolutely loves to do-- helping employees in transition find their passion and define their ideal work environment. Take This Job and Love It will resonate by building your hope, focus, energy and time on productive, faith-building efforts for visioning and then transitioning to a new career and work reality for you.

—Thomas Garrett
Global Fortune 500 CFO and Treasurer

In today's rapidly changing economy, it is essential to reskill and retrain for future career advancement. This book is specific to Goodwill's mission to transform people's lives through education and work.

—Kenny Hill
CEO, Goodwill Central Texas

Patti Nails It!!! The combination of her entrepreneurial and C-Suite career and extensive experience helping employees find their passion and define their ideal work environment makes her the perfect author for this book. "Take This Job and Love It" is a great guide for anyone looking for new opportunities in today's fast-changing labor market.

—Phillip B. Walker
Managing Partner
Career Partners International - Austin

Joining Patti's Executive Career Action Team connected me to a group of invaluable executive advisors as well as her high-energy and professional career transition coaching. By following the career search strategies outlined in "Take This Job and Love It, we successfully attracted and negotiated fulfilling and profitable new positions.

—Francisco Sacasa
President, Hire Better

After months of frustration applying for 1000s of jobs on the internet, I joined Patti's Executive Career Action Team. Not only was Patti's positivity and enthusiasm contagious, based on her recommendations, I changed my career search strategy to networking, and found a job in 4 weeks. This book lays out the groundwork for anyone like me who has had a stellar career trajectory, and never looked for a job before.

—Matthew Do
CPO, CeCe Veggie Co.

Take This Job and Love It demonstrates how anyone can create and attain a successful pathway to their career growth and advancement. It provides practical wisdom and advice garnered through Patti's extensive career coaching of thousands of Executives and C-Suite Professionals. This book combined with self-reflection on your strengths, interests and opportunities is an excellent tool for anyone looking for new opportunities and increased responsibilities in their companies.

—Ben Yaeger
Head of Sales, Marketing and
Corporate Development
RealManage

TRANSFORM YOUR JOB SEARCH

Patti Boyle

TRANSFORM YOUR JOB SEARCH

Library of Congress Cataloging-in-Publication Data

For permissions:
Patti Boyle patti@purepotentialconsulting.com
https://www.purepotentialconsulting.com

ISBN: 978-1-64184-363-8 (Paperback)
ISBN: 978-1-64184-364-5 (eBook)

You were born with potential.
You were born with goodness and trust. You
were born with ideals and dreams.
You were born with wings.
You are not meant for crawling.
So, Don't You Have Wings.
Learn to use them and fly.

Rumi

DEDICATION

This book is dedicated to my greatest teachers,

My late father, Ed Boyle and mother, Adele Boyle

To the thousands of jobs seekers whom I have been blessed to assist in finding the wisdom and courage to do what they love in alignment with their passions and life purpose.

ACKNOWLEDGEMENT

For years people told me I should write a book. After my company and I won several awards and received considerable media publicity, I was even offered a book contract. Even though I felt an inner urge to write a book, the timing never seemed right and the truth is I never seemed to make it a priority and find the time. Then one day the stars began to line up and I finally began to write my book.

Thank you, thank you, thank you to Bruce Campney, President of Hired Texas. I facilitated a Career Action Team for Senior Professionals between jobs. At the end of a meeting, Bruce handed me a mind map outlining the career advice I preached week after week. His mind map became the impetus and blueprint for this book. Many thanks to all members past and present of the executive and professional career action teams that I facilitate weekly. Your personal job searches contributed content for this book and your encouragement and support are deeply appreciated.

Special thanks to Tom Bird, my writing coach and publisher. Much appreciation to John Hodgkinson for his patience in holding my hand and mentoring me through the editing and publishing process.

In deepest gratitude to Denise Cassino, for her friendship and book coaching. She is an extremely dedicated and competent book marketing specialist. Her guidance has been invaluable. Without Denise's support, I would probably still be in the 81% of people who feel they have a book within them, yet do not write it, or the ones like me that write it, yet never publish it.

Much love and appreciation to my family and many friends who cheer me on through all my endeavors. Special shout out to my daughter Brittany and son Brian for their unconditional support always! The combination of Brittany's technology talent and "Just Do It" approach helped push me over the finish line and finally get my book to publishing.

CONTENTS

Chapter 1

DO YOU LOVE YOUR WORK?

American workers are feeling better about their career prospects as the economy improves and unemployment is lower. Yet most aren't thrilled about their actual jobs. According to Gallup's most recent State of American Workplace Report, there are currently more than 128.57 million employees working full-time in the American workforce. The percentage of "engaged" workers, those who love their jobs and make their organization and America better every day is now 34%, the highest level since Gallup began reporting the figure in 2000.

The percentage who are "actively disengaged" – workers who have miserable work experiences is now at its lowest level at 13%.

Even though this is the lowest on record, these employees can be a negative force in the workplace, with the potential to destroy the great work done by the "engaged" employees, as they tend to resent their jobs, complain, and drag down the morale of other employees.

The remaining 53% are not engaged at work—meaning they feel no connection to their jobs, thus they tend to do "bare minimum." They are just there. Gallup polls also show that this is not just an American phenomenon, only 13% of people worldwide actually like going to work. This is a disturbing number, to say the least, for both individuals and companies. Most employees aren't engaged in their jobs or emotionally invested in their work and are not focused on helping their organizations improve and grow.

In addition to a lack of engagement, a 2017 study by the Federal Reserve Bank of New York showed that of recent college graduates age 22-27, 4% are unemployed and 44% underemployed. Underemployed is settling for jobs that are not full-time, do not pay well, and in many cases do not require a college degree. For the first time in the modern era, the US Census Bureau reports that 40% of young people aged 18 to 34 are living with their parents.

Where are You in the Most Recent Statistics?

Do you wake up on Monday morning feeling alive and excited that it is another work week? Alternatively, do you suffer from Sunday syndrome, a sinking feeling that comes on late afternoon in anticipation of having to return to work on Monday? Do you feel like you have to go to work, or happy that you get to go to work?

There are many reasons you might choose to stay at a job you dislike:

- You need the salary.
- You believe there are no jobs for you.
- You think you don't have the skills, education or training to do what you want.
- You believe you are too young or too old.

No amount of pay or perceived security is worth the consequences. Being miserable with your job has significant adverse health consequences, impacts your personal life, lowers motivation and passion and lowers your confidence and self-worth.

All of us will go through tough times that we don't understand in our lives and careers. Take This Job and Love It! is intended to help anyone settling or navigating transitions in their lifework.

Whether you are unemployed, underemployed or unhappily employed, it is time to revision, redesign, and recreate your career.

I believe everyone has a dream and a life calling.

You deserve to be doing what you love, loving what you do, and making the money you desire in doing so.

Take This Job and Love It! is a guide to see lifework challenges as calls to evolve and grow, to develop resiliency, to align with your True Self, and to attract new possibilities and right livelihood.

In overcoming adversity in my own life, I discovered what I loved to do, then turned my passion into a multi-million-dollar company. Helping hundreds of global corporations navigate change and transition, and thousands of people recreate their lifework and find meaningful and purposeful new opportunities is my passion and profession.

Chapter 2

CALLING IN YOUR CALLING

"Your profession is not what brings home your weekly paycheck, your profession is what you're put here on earth to do with such passion and intensity that it becomes spiritual in calling."

~ Vincent van Gogh

Whether you are currently in school, working full-time or part-time, between jobs, contemplating a change or even approaching retirement, there is a calling within each of us to make a difference. We sometimes think that to make a difference in the world

5

we must be worldly souls like Mother Teresa, Gandhi, Martin Luther King, or Nelson Mandela.

YouTube of Admiral William H. McRaven's commencement speech given to the University of Texas' graduating class of 2014 that went viral is very inspiring, I recommend taking the time to look it up.

Admiral McRaven began by simplifying for the graduates how each of them could potentially change the world. Quoting statistics from askme.com, he stated that the average person will physically meet 10,000 people in their lifetime, and, "If of those 10,000, each person positively impacted and changed the lives of ten people, and those people each changed the lives of another ten, after five generations (or about 140 years) the lives of 800 million people would change for the better." After one more generation, the lives of every person on earth would change for the better.

When you attend the memorial services of most people who live into their 90's or beyond, the ten people they have impacted for the better, or in some cases worse, are all there. It is their family members.

It's incredible to think that you spend more time on a daily basis with the people you work with than your own families, unless you work in a family business or from the home, side by side with your spouse, partner, parent or children. The opportunity to significantly impact others and change lives for the better exists in our workplaces and businesses.

Not only can our companies' product or services positively impact lives, how we treat our fellow employees, customers, vendors and other key stakeholders can change lives.

We can change the world simply by showing up and being a beneficial presence to someone in our workplace. What if you considered positively impacting just one person monthly through your work? Think over the span of your entire career, how many lives would be positively affected?

Through our lifework, we not only bring meaning and purpose to our own lives, but we also have the opportunity to change the lives of others. Martin Luther King Jr. said; "Whatever your life's work is, do it well. Even if it does not fall in the category of one of the so-called big professions, do it well. As one college president said, 'A man should do his job so well that the living, the dead, and the unborn could do it no better.' If it falls your lot to be a street sweeper, sweep streets like Michelangelo painted pictures, like Shakespeare wrote poetry, like Beethoven composed music; sweep streets so well that all the host of Heaven and earth will have to pause and say, 'Here lived a great street sweeper, who swept his job well.'"

This is the difference between a career and calling? Your career refers to the service you perform using your knowledge, skills, talents, and strengths in exchange for a salary or other income and benefits. You might see it as your job, profession, employment, work, livelihood, occupation, making a living, trade, vocation or "just a job." Usually, the primary motive for going to work every day is to earn an income to provide for yourself and your family.

Your calling refers to your passion, inclination, personal interests, and is usually aligned with higher order. We often hear clergy, military, environmentalists or mothers raising children speak of having a calling. It isn't just something you want to do. It is something you need to do, something that touches you deeply and captures your imagination. You may not be able to explain why.

A calling may or may not earn an income. The primary difference between a career and a calling is that a career is a job done primarily for profit. A calling can be very profitable, and is generally for innate satisfaction, fulfillment, meaning, and significance.

Why not consider overlapping your career and your calling and having both total appreciation and income in your work life? What could be more fun than to love what you do, and to feel what you do matters, while earning the money you desire?

The Journey to My Calling

"The only way to do great work is to love what you do. If you haven't found it yet, keep looking. Don't Settle."

~ Steve Jobs

Visiting Houston always brings back memories of the warmth, joy and full circle of coming home to my True Self. It was in Houston that a small-town girl from an Irish/Italian immigrant family and mining town in Montana was able to launch out of education as a teacher and administrator and start a business. My business helped Fortune 500 corporations and their employees navigate transitions due to downsizings, mergers, acquisitions, declining oil prices, losing funding for aerospace projects, or merely realigning their business strategies.

It was in Houston that my career and calling overlapped. I left a secure position as a university administrator and teacher, and within three years of starting my business, Career Visions Inc., it grew and expanded it into a multi-million-dollar venture with thirty offices, employing over 150 employees nationwide.

It appeared to most people, including myself at the time, that I was an overnight success. I did not realize then that my career and calling had intersected and become one.

Invariably, people would point out how lucky I was and how fortunate I must have been to be in the right place at the right time. Countless news reporters would be onsite when Career Visions or I won numerous awards, including being named the Second Fastest Growing Privately Held Company in Houston three years after start-up, being named Small Businessperson of the Year, or Houston Supplier of the Year for delivering high-quality, exceptional services to a fast-growing list of Corporate America's largest companies.

Every award Career Visions or I won, the news reporters would line up with microphones in my face asking the same question:

"How does a schoolteacher grow a business to a multi-million-dollar venture in less than five years?"

A Houston newspaper and a local news channel both reported after one award ceremony that I refused to answer this question. I didn't refuse to answer the question - they refused to print my answer. I thanked God and my staff for Career Visions' success.

Even in those days, the constant negative news didn't want to credit God for anything or report a positive and inspirational story. If there was any luck involved in this venture, my entrepreneurial success was the result of having attracted the right opportunities and the right staff with differing and unique gifts, skills, and abilities to grow Career Visions.

Today, I would be considered a "millennial entrepreneur" who hired many employees, who would be classified as "baby boomers," with the wisdom and proven business experience to grow Career Visions and handle me at the same time.

When I started my business, I had a lot of energy, passion, and drive, yet I now realize I was young, dumb and inexperienced. Fortunately, I was coachable.

At that time, I turned down a book contract offer to write my story of how I went from a young educational administrator and teacher to starting and growing Career Vision. I was flattered but rejected the proposal as it would have been a concise story, or probably edited and rewritten as a standard business textbook by a publishing company. I could not provide them with a business or marketing plan, the name of my PR or marketing firm, where I finished my MBA or obtained my business experience.

At that time, I had none of the above, only a title, "I Didn't Do It, God Did."

"Oh, By the Way, God Also Provided Me with an Exceptional Staff and the Right Opportunities," was the subtitle.

Prov. 3: 5 & 6 says, "Trust in the LORD with all your heart, and do not lean on your own understanding. In all your ways acknowledge him, and he will make straight your paths".

I now realize that in the midst of one of the most traumatic and turbulent times in my life, I followed God's path and was pulled by a vision, or "calling," to uplift individuals who thought they had cradle to grave employment, that they would retire from a company with a gold watch and live happily ever after.

Ironically, after years of helping thousands of employees deal with the loss of their jobs and often time many life losses, I faced numerous traumatic experiences and personal losses that left me paralyzed with grief and pain.

I now understand these tough times were prerequisites for me to step into the fullness of my destiny.

Chapter 3

DARK NIGHTS OF THE SOUL

"Grief is often defined as the normal and natural emotional reaction to loss or change of any kind".

I n 1988, my perfect Barbie-doll lifestyle was challenged and disrupted by the sudden death of my father. We spent Christmas in Montana, and it was apparent to my parents that both me and my marriage were falling apart. My former husband lived in Houston, and I was living in Lafayette, Louisiana and juggling many balls. I was a calculus teacher and handling all the student activities at the private high school where I was employed, raising a four-year old and six-year old by myself, and many weekends drove over 200 miles to see my former husband in Houston.

In the previous June my father had taken early retirement from his twenty-five-year career in education, so he decided to fly back to Lafayette with me. My parents had never been apart in their thirty-three years of marriage. My mother had not retired yet, and encouraged my father to help me and enjoy the warmer weather of the south versus persevering in the frigid temperatures and snow. I loved having my father with me for the last six weeks of his life. His companionship, wisdom, and support to the children and me helped as day by day I regained my strength and optimism.

I would return from work to the laughter of my children playing with him and an excellent dinner that he had prepared. As he helped to add joy to our household, I began to regain the weight I had lost. He also enjoyed the warmer weather, a few days a week he would golf with my neighbors. The final weekend of his life, we attended the celebration of two Mardi Gras Balls in Louisiana. Whilst my mother loved to dance, my father never really enjoyed it, and yet my girlfriends had him out on the dance floor in typical Louisiana party spirit, dancing every dance.

He planned to fly back to Montana and had booked an early flight the following Tuesday morning. That worked, as I expected to drive him to the airport, drop my children off at school, and go to my work. We talked all the way to the airport, and he and my mom planned to return at Easter to help me with my move to Houston. As we entered the airport, he started to feel ill and went to the restroom. When he came out, he said maybe he had food poising from the Mexican restaurant the night before.

Even though we had checked his luggage in already, it was apparent he was not well enough to get on the plane. I looked in the back seat at my four-year old son, Brian, and as I looked forward, my father's head fell on my lap. Somehow on total autopilot, I was able to get to the closest hospital. I remember jumping out of my car, running into the emergency exit and screaming, "Help me! Help me! My father has passed out."

Brian, who was in the back seat during this entire tragedy, had to tell the hospital staff our names and where I worked.

I was in total shock when they said to me my father did not make it, he had died of a heart attack. I remember going through all the initial stages of grief, bargaining, crying hysterically, No, No, No. I felt disbelief and denial, feeling this was a bad dream and eventually I would wake up. I remember my last fond memory of my father, walking into the airport holding my son

Brian's little hand as they talked to each other, and my son repeatedly asking my father why he was leaving and asking him to stay with us.

My most profound remembrance was walking out of the hospital after my father's sudden passing with a shoe box containing his wallet, eyeglasses, and keys. I continually stared at the shoe box in disbelief. I remember thinking how ironic it is that at the end of our lives, none of our material possessions have value or go with us.

Years later, on a visit to China, I thought about the shoebox. I visited the tombs of emperors whose wives, concubines and worldly possessions were all buried with them. I had heard the saying, live every day like it is your last. That day I fully understood what that meant.

For the next year, I found myself in profound sadness whenever I stopped moving and wasn't actively doing something. So, I just kept running. Today there is more of an awareness of how trauma affects us emotionally and physically. It even has a diagnosis, Post Traumatic Stress Disorder (PTSD). Rather than PTSD, this event launched me into Post Traumatic Growth.

Within three years of my father's sudden death, I had moved to Houston, left education and started my business, Career Visions Inc. Amidst my marriage crumbling and the impending divorce, I suffered a compounding loss. My rites as a devout Catholic to serve as a Liturgical Minister and Eucharistic Minister were revoked due to my separation. My life was reorganizing on every level.

Additionally, my ten-year old daughter was in MD Anderson Cancer Center undergoing tests for a tumor that the doctors feared may attach to her brain. Homeschooling her and running my business from there was a juggling act, as you can imagine.

My ministry in the world moved to produce significant revenue for my company, serving as a "corporate hospice worker" in some of the top boardrooms of Fortune 10 companies around the globe. I had the opportunity to educate Executive Management and Senior Human Resource teams. I didn't realize at the time, but it was my personal experience with the emotions of my multiple changes and losses that prepared me to understand how these employees felt and reacted. I knew firsthand the importance of treating them with sensitivity and care. These events propelled my career and calling to overlap.

I was in the zone, doing what I loved, loving what I was doing, and helping significant organizations and tens of thousands of people transform their job losses into opportunities - and making millions doing so.

My post-traumatic expertise not only unleashed my passion. It qualified me to train and coach executives and managers to develop career tracks and strategies, to set performance goals, lay- off, fire, terminate or sever employees. Being prepared, anticipating and dealing with the emotions and reactions of Post Traumatic Shock that employees experienced, particularly long- term ones, was the first step. I trained and empowered company executives, HR, and career coaches to understand the grief cycle. I recognized that employees who were severed needed assistance to move through their career losses and develop a new vision to attract new career opportunities.

When I tell people what I do for a living, they immediately chuckle and say, "Oh, like George Clooney in his movie Up in the Air?"

My response, "No, exactly the opposite."

The function may have been the same, dealing with massive downsizings and thousands of employees losing their jobs in one day, however Career Visions' methodology and coaching was precisely the opposite.

First, we familiarized CEOs, their executive teams and managers with the emotional roller coaster that is grief by Elizabeth Kűbler-Ross and enlightened them to the fact that the employee would go through many of the same emotions as someone who just lost a loved one. Elizabeth Kűbler-Ross, a pioneer in the loss and grief recovery movement, gained her experience working with terminally ill patients and their families. Research has found that the same cycle and emotions apply to any significant loss, including a job. I knew the feelings of this grief and loss cycle well from my experience with my father's sudden death.

Understanding the grief and loss cycle spring-boarded me into transferring my Divine skills, gifts talents and strengths into starting a business to help organizations and employees deal with their emotions when the sudden change happened.

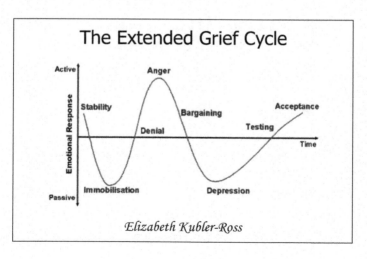

The Extended Grief Cycle

Elizabeth Kubler-Ross

- **Shock** – Initial paralysis of hearing bad news and feeling immobilized.
- **Denial** – Refusing to believe what has happened, feeling shocked.
  - o "This can't be happening."
- **Anger** – Accusing others, such as a supreme being, friends and bosses, colleagues of what has occurred.
  - o "How dare you let this happen/do this to me!"
- **Bargaining** – Asking for just one more chance and seeking, in vain, a way out.
- **Depression** – Experiencing listlessness or exhaustion, combined with feelings of helplessness, guilt or lack of interest in life.
  - o "I might as well give up."
- **Acceptance** – Facing the loss and moving on, returning to setting goals in your life and focusing your energy more positively.
  - o "I'm ready to deal with this now."
- **Action**

Almost everyone is familiar with the fight-flight response – your reaction to a stimulus or event perceived as an imminent threat to your survival. However, less well known is the fight-flight-freeze response, which adds a crucial dimension to how you are likely to react when a situation confronting you overwhelms you, and you feel paralyzed with fear. When we experience an unwelcome or traumatic event, individuals will fall into one or more of these patterns.

John W. James and Russell Friedman, founders of the Grief Recovery Method define grief as "The conflicting feelings caused by the end of or change in a familiar pattern or behavior".

Job loss of any kind including retirement triggers grief for many. Research shows that losing or leaving a job can be as traumatic as losing a loved one or going through a divorce.

After an employee found out about a pending or actual job loss or demotion or decided on retirement, we wanted to meet with the employee as soon as possible to help them with next steps.

Dealing with their emotions, accepting that their job was over or changing, and getting them into a process of visioning the possibility of attracting a new opportunity was imperative.

The higher your resiliency and ability to envision new options and possibilities, the greater your ability to move forward and create a life you love living.

Staying stuck in any or a combination of fight-flight-freeze responses can lead you to a downward spiral into a life of suffering, pain and even health challenges.

Fight

When training managers on how to tell an employee that their job situation is changing, I found they usually anticipated and feared the fight response more than any other reaction. The worst- case scenario is the post office killer. It is the least likely to occur, and in most situations, can be anticipated or predicted. Individuals who exhibit this reaction typically have shown the behavior in the past.

The fight response occurs when you hear unwelcome or traumatic news and begin to cry, or get angry and burst into rage. This stimulus produces emotion - crying, fight in the eyes, glaring stares, and loudness in the voice. Metaphors like a bomb just went off best describe this response. In such instances, the hormones released into the sympathetic nervous system, especially adrenaline, prime you to do battle and defeat the enemy. It is the reaction of Weepy William/Wilma or Hot Head Harry/Henrietta. Techniques for remaining calm and not feeling anxious or distressed are best in dealing with this response.

Flight

Conversely, if you view the challenge or situation as too powerful to overcome, the urge is to run faster and faster. This is how I dealt with the trauma of my father's death, I just kept moving from one activity to the next. Anxiety, shallow-breathing, leg/foot movement and darting eyes are ways of identifying this response to trauma and adversity.

Pain is unavoidable, suffering is not. Suffering comes from trying to avoid feelings. A few daily practices to slow down, to calm anxiety and distress, include deep breathing, walking, stretching, writing, yoga, talking, or listening to music.

Freeze

Have you ever been so immobilized by fear that you merely dissociated from it all? Freeze is the disabling response that happens in seconds. You neither defeat the frightening challenge or opposition, nor run from it. This self-paralyzing reaction causes you to feel numb or stuck. There is a sense of dread, your breath is restricted, and your heart is pounding.

How you react to unwelcome news or adversity in life situations in the past may be indicative of how you will respond to current or future setbacks or losses. Awareness is the key to learning from your reactions and developing different coping strategies.

Exercise

What is your "go-to" reaction to past set-backs, significant changes or sudden losses? Understanding your "go-to" responses may help you to overcome current challenges. Is it fight-flight-freeze or a combination?

Take several minutes now to write about your reactions to setbacks, significant changes or sudden losses.

List 5 significant changes, setbacks or losses in your life.

1. Select the most significant one for you and briefly describe: Who? What? When? Where?
2. How did it feel when you were experiencing it?
3. What was your stress response?
   Fight – Flight – Freeze.
4. How do you feel about it now?
5. What did you learn from the experience?

6. What resources (knowledge, skills, wisdom) do you now have as a result of the experience?
7. How might you use these resources to help cope with your current setbacks or transitions?

Chapter 4

TRANSITIONS

"Not in his goals but in his transitions,
man is great."

~ Ralph Waldo Emerson

C areer resiliency is being able to let go of fear from the past and recreate your life and vision possibilities again. The Chinese symbol for CRISIS is the same for danger as it is for an opportunity.

In every seeming crisis, the most challenging part of the process is letting go of the old situation and way of being and visioning, seeing and feeling new opportunities and possibilities vs. dwelling in the thoughts of DANGER, and rerunning worse case scenarios over and over.

What dangers and opportunities does change represent for you at this point in your life and career?

Danger	Opportunities
Financial worries	Find new possibilities for income
Family stress	Increased Career Satisfaction
Not knowing the future	Defining a new future
Loss of colleagues and friends	Find new ways to meet people
Lack of structure and security	Creating new structures and security
Feeling outdated	Learning something new
Loss of purpose	Renewed sense of purpose
Feeling rejected	Creating conditions for acceptance

Other:

The real danger is, what if you don't get into action and use your Divine gifts, skills, and talents to make a difference in the world?

Research shows that a frightening percentage of early retirees develop significant illnesses, or even die, within eighteen months of retirement or leaving a company. That was the case with my father, he retired in June and died nine months later. I had sometimes wondered, what if someone had helped him to develop a life plan before he retired that included a Vision of how many people he could still help? No longer did he have to work for money, retirement and social security guaranteed him a higher income for life than he had made as an educator.

Today, a large number of baby boomers are either forced out of the workplace or leave their companies in their fifties and early sixties with much wisdom, knowledge, energy and perfect health. Art Markman, a neuroscientist, reports that our brains function at peak performance in our twenties. But, our actual wisdom peaks at age sixty-eight.

Regardless of your age, you deserve to work with passion, purpose and productivity, with profits not only ongoing but also expanding. It is essential to understand the stages of transition.

The late Bill Bridges, author of Transitions: Making Sense of Life Changes, described three overlapping stages of transition - the ending, the neutral zone and the new beginning. He went on to say, "In the modern age of instantaneous gratification we think that the new beginning should occur immediately just like turning on a light switch. It is no wonder that even though we have to deal with changes all our lives, most of us take them poorly."

"In the neutral zone, we feel unproductive; we are dealing with the emotional roller coaster of emotions. Throughout history we read accounts of wisdom leaders like Jesus, Moses, Buddha, Mohammad, Dante and countless saints and sages that withdrew and returned, only to be reborn again."

Like any life changes, a successful career or job transitions include the following three overlapping phases.

Ending

On the day of significant downsizing, Career Visions' staff would be onsite to coordinate large- scale downsizings where thousands of people would be laid off in a short period. One day a company laid off 13,000 people on the same day around the country.

These days are endings for every one of those thousands of people. It is a stressful day for the leaders of the company, the managers, the employees being affected, the survivors and even our staff.

There are so many losses attached to job loss, particularly for employees who have been at companies for decades and those who have served in senior positions and made higher salaries. They have lost their jobs and source of income, yet the most significant loss is often their identity. Many employees, and all of us to some degree, identify ourselves with our job titles versus who we indeed are. Job titles can become our identities.

Additionally, their fellow employees are their friends and support system. In some cases, they have spent as much or more time with their colleagues over the years than with their own families. A significant adjustment is the loss of their structure and schedule - they get up at the same time, have lunch at the same time and generally commute the same route.

This is the period when you disengage from your old work identity and memories. Tasks for this phase includes saying goodbye, cleaning out things that remind you of your former workplace, and admitting that this chapter of your life is over.

As a career coach, the first challenge is to help employees let go of defining themselves as their job titles.

Neutral Zone

Amazingly, after the outplaced employees reconcile the shock and reality of the situation in the neutral zone, the job loss was a blessing for a large number who had settled in jobs that were stressful or no longer challenged them. Often, they were "settling" for a paycheck, restrained by "golden handcuffs," or waiting for a possible pension in the future. It is an opportunity to move out of their comfort zone, find a new job, or learn something new and stop settling for discontentment and mediocracy.

The neutral zone is the in-between period where you might find yourself disoriented, confused and directionless. Actions that help you move through this stage are visioning, self-assessment, seeking information, surrounding yourself with supportive friends, family, and confidants, gaining control and reconsidering your sense of power in your life and work. It is also the time when creativity soars.

New Beginning

When I was overseeing large-scale layoffs, and 500 to 15,000 employees lost their jobs, sometimes within a few months, I was often asked, "Wow, how do you do it? Isn't it depressing to see all those people fired?"

Rather than seeing them as "fired," I saw them as having an opportunity to get "fired up" about their life and work again. It was a new beginning, a chance to vision and attract new opportunities.

Because of my own experience, I viewed them as the chosen ones who got the chance to redesign their life and work and come alive again. I knew the job loss in most cases was an undisguised blessing. Life is not over when a job with a title, a paycheck and benefits end. Job loss is merely a wakeup call and an excellent opportunity to go within, an opportunity to reevaluate what you really like to do, put a plan together, get out and talk to people doing what you want to do, and attract new possibilities and opportunities using your unique strengths, gifts, skills and talents.

Creating a new sense of structure and purpose is essential. As you begin to move forward, you will attract new opportunities and situations. Once again, you will feel energetic, alive, engaged, and productive.

Chapter 5

CROSSROADS

*"If you can't change the situation,
change yourself."*

~ Viktor Frankl

In addition to all the personal losses I was experiencing, the sudden loss of my father, my marriage unraveling and my daughter's illness, my career also took an unexpected turn for the worse. When we moved to Houston in March, I left my position teaching gifted and talented students and serving as an administrator in a Catholic High School in Louisiana. The school provided a safe, loving, supportive and nurtured workplace and environment.

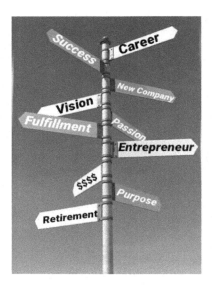

It was quite a culture shock when I accepted a teaching position in a public high school in an upper-middle-class suburb in Houston. I left dedicated colleagues who supported each other and were committed to their students. In fact, three were at the hospital with me when my father passed. We were family, a committed team of professionals who strived to provide superior guidance and support for the students whether it be sports, speech events or math fairs. Our students were motivated by their families and the school to excel at everything they did. In the last AP class that I taught at the private high school, nine of the eleven students were National Merit Finalists.

You can imagine my confusion on my first day of work, walking into the teacher's lounge of the Houston public high school to find it filled with negativity, burnout, and apathy. Each week I heard, "Oh no, it's Monday," Wednesday was "hump day," and, "thank God it's Friday."

I was confused the second day, when the teachers gathered and held their daily ritual of marking off one more day until the end of the year on a large calendar prominently displayed on the wall. Many of the teachers were tenured and even had calendars on their desks counting down their time until retirement.

When my dad was with me the last weeks of his life, he would comment daily on how happy I was as an educator, how much I enjoyed what I did, and how much my students and the parents liked me. I had always loved my work, even in college, and had no idea that over 54% of employees settle for jobs they are miserable in or don't find fulfilling. I had been a cultural fit for the organizations I worked with, my values and work ethic were a match.

The final quarter of the year, I chose to avoid the negativity by staying out of the griping and complaining in the teacher's lounge. The most significant discipline issues I had experienced in the Catholic High School were that the girls sometimes hiked their school uniform and chewed gum, and the most critical offense was an occasional cigarette in the restrooms. In the public high school, it felt like a free-for-all to me. Drug busts, food fights and brawls in the cafeteria, fights, and unmotivated and unruly behavior in the classroom.

Two months into this assignment, during final exams, I turned around only to have a student pointing a gun at me. It was one of the most frightening experiences of my life. I did not realize what was happening to me was really happening for me.

As Oprah says, "All negative energy is seeking a solution." When faced with these situations she asks herself three questions:

1. What is it here to teach me?
2. Am I able to solve the problem?
3. Is it time to move on?

I realized that it was time to move on. As Yogi Berra says, "When you come to a fork in the road take it." I decided to resign from my seemingly secure teaching position and paycheck at the end of the year. It took courage to say, "I want to make my path, I want to dream again, I want to find work that celebrates me." Recovering from multiple adversities simultaneously required courage, resiliency, and to get out of my comfort zone. As Mary Manin Morrissey, author of Building Your Field of Dreams said, "Our discontent is a gift from Spirit."

Divine Discontent is the generator that gives us the power to act on our dreams. We learn and grow through challenges, and every adversity that I have experienced had a hidden gift. Whether you are unemployed, underemployed, or unhappily employed, embrace and accept that this is a gift calling you to evolve, grow and act on your dreams.

Chapter 6

MOVE OUT OF YOUR COMFORT ZONE

"A dream is your creative vision for your life in the future. You must break out of your current comfort zone and become comfortable with the unfamiliar and unknown."

~ Denis Waitley

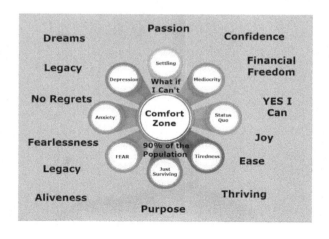

When individuals lose their jobs and finally begin to visualize future possibilities, they often recognize how fortunate they are in comparison to their former colleagues who are unhappily employed and caught in the chaos and disruption of a corporate reorganization. The Career Visions staff was fortunate to experience the other side of the equation when outplaced employees went back to school to upgrade their skills, found meaningful and purposeful new careers, and in many cases even increased their salaries.

Yes, finding a new job and growing your salary is a possibility, I have seen thousands of job seekers do so. Finding a fulfilling, satisfying, uplifting new opportunity is the real benefit.

Sometimes when difficult or challenging situations or losses arise in our lives, what appears to be happening to us is happening for us. In the tough times, it is a chance to remember your dream.

There are many stories of people who, because of setbacks, life changes or traumatic events, get out of their comfort zone.

One of my favorite stories is Harland Sanders, founder of the restaurant chain Kentucky Fried Chicken (KFC). At age five, his father died. At age sixteen he quit school, and by seventeen he had already lost four jobs. Married at eighteen,

Harland became a father at nineteen, before his wife left him a year later and took their baby daughter. At age twenty-two he joined the army and was washed out there. He applied for law school, was rejected, became an insurance salesman - another failure to be added to his resume. After rejection after rejection, he became a cook and a dishwasher in a small café and retired from there at age sixty-five. On the first day of his retirement, he received his first social security check from the government for $105.

Feeling like a total failure, he decided to commit suicide and sat under a tree writing his will. Then suddenly, instead of a suicide note, he thought of writing what he would have accomplished if he had the choice to start his life over. He realized there was much more that he hadn't done yet. There was one thing he could do better than anyone else - he cooked the best chicken anyone had ever tasted.

So, he borrowed $87 to buy a fryer and his recipe ingredients and went door to door selling licenses to his unique chicken recipe. He went door to door selling it to his neighbors in Kentucky as well as to license it to restaurants. He was rejected yet again, 1009 times from the restaurants he tried to sell his recipe to. The

1010th restaurant gave him the YES moment. KFC was born.

Remember at age sixty-five he was ready to commit suicide, yet by age eighty-eight he had built an empire and become a billionaire. Now KFC is one of the largest restaurant chains with almost 20,000 locations globally in 123 countries.

Regardless of your age, what is your chicken recipe? What is the one thing you do better than anyone else that you know?

Another example is John Walsh, an American television personality, criminal investigator, human rights and victim rights advocate and host/creator of America's Most Wanted. John became an anti-crime advocate following the murder of his son, Adam. Before Adam's death, John worked in building high-end luxury hotels and was an executive for a resort and casino in the Bahamas. John transferred his executive and management skills to advocating and helping other victim's families and solving crimes. Walsh's net worth totals over $10 million.

Lee Iacocca turned around Chrysler and became its most famous CEO, five years after being fired from Ford. I have countless stories from my years in the career transition and outplacement business of employees who lost their jobs to find themselves. As a result of losing their jobs, they discovered their callings and found meaning, purpose, and money doing what they loved.

When I started my company, as I mentioned, I would have been considered a Millennial and my first employee would be considered a Baby Boomer today.

Culver was fifty-eight years old and a former president of a bank. He was severed when his bank was acquired by a larger bank. Educated in business and graduated in law, Culver received an award as one of Houston's Greater Communicators of the Year and served as a deacon in a large Houston Church. Politically connected throughout Texas and the country, his father was an Assistant DA in Dallas when JFK was killed.

When he was taking computer classes in the university program that I directed, I would notice that sometimes the line in front of his door was longer than our trained and salaried career counselors. One day I stopped by and asked him if all the job seekers asking for his advice was distracting.

"No, quite the contrary, it actually uplifts my Spirit," he told me, "I could be at an upscale outplacement center. I chose the university program because I knew I needed to learn how to use the computer now that I don't have a secretary. Now I see I can help a lot of people."

He went on to say, "For some reason, my friends always sent their kids to me for job search advice when they were getting out of college. Helping people find jobs is something I love to do."

While Culver was retraining and improving his computer skills by day, I could see he was doing career coaching with other unemployed professionals and executives in the program. So, fortunately, my first employee was Culver. He knew how to operate a company. I did not. Culver taught me how to run my business, how to read a balance sheet and income statement, and enthusiastically encouraged me to take business classes. Eventually he encouraged me to enroll in the three-year executive Entrepreneurial Leadership Program sponsored by Inc. magazine, YEO and MIT's Sloan School of Business.

In addition to be my business coach and trusted advisor, he coached and helped thousands of executive job seekers secure new employment. Culver once told me that this was the best job he had ever had. He said it didn't feel like a job to him, it felt more like a ministry. Despite his long resume of highly impressive positions with highly impressive companies, Culver had found his calling.

In the process, Culver, along with other executives I hired from the university's Executive Career Transition and Retraining Center, taught me what I did not know, how to grow and run a business. This has been an invaluable lesson for me in everything I do. I learned to do what I do well. I learned to hire and surround myself with the right people to do what I did not like or know how to do, nor did I care to learn how to do it. Together, we touched the lives of people in need of help and made a difference.

In addition to hiring senior leaders for Career Visions and watching them find passion and fulfillment in their work lives, I have been honored to help unemployed, unhappily employed and underemployed individuals follow their heart, dare to dream big and overlap their careers and callings.

In one corporate downsizing in San Francisco, I had the opportunity to coach Ann. She was a petroleum engineer. When she lost her job, we first began by doing a battery of career and self- assessments. To my surprise, Ann's interests seemed to resemble an artist with high creativity and visual acuity.

When I asked Ann where this came from, she said, "When I was a child, I loved sitting on the floor dressing and redressing my dolls." She told of losing herself in this activity for hours, and her parents would have to insist that she stop and go to bed. In her early teens, she even took sewing classes and would make clothes for her dolls. When I asked how she decided to go to engineering school, she said, "My father was an engineer and executive in a large oil company. I always wanted to go to college and study fashion merchandising, but he insisted that was not a profession and that I would not make any money."

Following his guidance, she followed in his footsteps, became an engineer, and for six years struggled through her career unhappy and unfulfilled. When she lost her job as a result of declining oil prices and foreign competition, part of her severance package included federal educational assistance. She took advantage of the federal assistance, and left San Francisco to attend the Fashion Institute of Technology in New York, one of the most recognized colleges for fashion, design and business. Five- years later she had learned new skills and transferred existing skills into a career she loved. She was a merchandising and design manager and making twice her engineering salary.

When I ventured out of the university and started Career Visions, there were corporate projects that the career coaches were still completing at the university. The Dean of the college blessed my move into my own business but asked me not to take the career counselors with me until all the funded projects ended.

There were several political problems with the career transition and retraining center at the University of Houston. First, it was receiving two million dollars of state and federal funding to help people who had lost jobs. The major problem was that because many of the oil companies were also funding the programs, it attracted executives and senior professionals. The average salary of the individuals we served was $70,000, and this was the early nineties. The sooner we could help these long-term employees develop a lifework plan, retrain and get back to work, the sooner they paid taxes again.

Additionally, these people had paid considerable taxes to receive the unemployment benefits and services they were receiving. Unfortunately, that is not how our government seems to want to fund programs. Unless someone is in need or poverty, they do not see they need financial help. I was young and politically naïve; the center's state and federal funding was in jeopardy even though participants were re-employed and back in the workforce in an average of four months. The program started to earn recognition as a best practice program for helping employees find jobs and was attracting attention from companies across the nation. It should have been a perfect model, business, government and education all working together to help with a central campaign issue every four years, finding people jobs.

During the past presidential election there was even a term coined, "the forgotten man or woman," and this became a central campaign promise, to help people find jobs. These "forgotten men or women" are the incredibly talented, hard-working people who have fallen out of the labor market because technology is changing our workforce so rapidly that constant lifework planning and retraining is essential for seasoned employees. In most cases, these employees become so disillusioned that they forget themselves and their own inner genius. For every job title that is being eliminated, new job titles are emerging. While mainframes have been replaced by laptops and even our cellphones, new opportunities in cybersecurity and artificial intelligence is emerging.

In a voluntary corporate downsizing at a chemical plant in West Texas, a safety manager named Joe had always liked his job. In his situation, he not only qualified for early retirement, his company provided $5000 of educational assistance and career and educational counseling as part of the voluntary severance package as an incentive to encourage employees to retire early. Joe always wanted to be a teacher and coach but didn't feel there was enough money in education when he went to college, so he studied math and science instead. John decided to take the voluntary severance package. For one year he lived on some of the severance monies the company provided and become a certified Math and PE teacher in the state of Texas. Two state football championships later, Joe not only loved and enjoyed a fulfilling and satisfying career in education and touched the lives of hundreds of young, he now collected two pensions.

Chapter 7

UPPER LIMITS

Conquer Your Hidden Fear and Take Life to the Next Level

You are only confined by the walls you build yourself. In Gay Hendricks' book The Big Leap, he speaks of our upper limits, or hidden fears that keep us stuck. Our upper limits are the limits that we are unconsciously programed to believe as children. Some psychologists believe that by age eight, many of our perceptions of life are no longer ours, they are the stories of our key influencers, our parents, grandparents, teachers, religious leaders and the communities we live in.

These programmed beliefs shape our attitudes, our attitudes drive our behaviors, and our behaviors become our habits. This habitual thinking becomes the upper limit of what we believe to be true and how we perceive we should act. The thought of being the first Catholic divorcee in my family totally blew the lid off the upper limits of my family and religious upbringing. Yet one of the last things my father said to me the night before he died was, "If you are staying in this marriage because we are Catholic, don't."

It was as though he knew this was his last advice to me and that he was giving me permission to break the upper limit of my Catholic upbringing, which said, "No divorce, no matter how unhappy you are or how bad it is on you, your spouse and the children physically, emotionally and Spiritually."

Leaving teaching was also a Big Leap for me. I had a bachelors and master's in education and loved my job as an educator for over ten years. It was what my father did for years as the first educated person in our family, and teaching was how he provided for our family. He retired securely with a full pension as did my grandfathers.

Obtaining tenure and retiring securely with a pension in hand was the upper limit of how I was raised to believe we should work and live. However, it was not the upper limit of my soul.

Exercise: What are your Upper Limits? Write them down.

Feel the Fear and Do It Anyway

*"The future belongs to those who believe
in the beauty of their dreams."*

~ *Eleanor Roosevelt*

I was working at a university when opportunities presented themselves to help companies design programs for employees who were displaced from their jobs due to corporate change, mergers, acquisitions, downsizings, and rightsizings. At that time, it was rare for professionals to be laid off, and their mentality was cradle-to-grave employment. Their fathers and grandfathers had worked for companies their entire lives and retired with the gold watch after thirty to forty years of working for the same company. I had the opportunity with my staff to design Career Transition Programs and retrain these employees for jobs within their own companies, or even more frightening, to help them transition out of the comfort of companies they had been employed with for years and find employment with another company. The programs we designed and offered to many Fortune 500 companies with headquarters or regional headquarters in the Houston area began to attract nationwide attention.

This accelerated when the National Business Employment Weekly wrote an article and cited the program as a best practice in the emerging growth field of outplacement. The national attention and publicity made it clear that large outplacement projects, helping companies outside the Houston Metro area, and taking in large sums of money without writing grants, was not part of the vision, mission or strategic intent of the university.

I remember one day walking into the Dean's office with a check for $225,000 from a multinational electronic data systems company. The company was restructuring and wanted us to manage their reorganization and help their employees.

"What are we supposed to do with this check. Did you even write a grant for it?" the Dean shouted. I said no, I just went and talked to the company about how we could help them. I then jokingly turned the check over and told him he could sign the check over to me, but he didn't find this at all funny.

This is the point that I knew my own job, and that of 100+ trainers, career counselors and administrative professionals, was on the line. The Dean called me in one day and told me that he wanted me to start winding down the Career Transition and Retraining Centers and stop taking projects. This was September, and he gave me until June to finish the remaining projects and close the center. He mentioned to me that I could probably stay on teaching classes because my teaching evaluations always came in so high, and he had a few other small grants that I could possibly manage. This felt safe and comfortable to me. My education and entire career were in administration and teaching. I also felt a sense of obligation to the companies we were serving and the employees and contractors who worked for me. Yet something in my gut told me that my time in education was coming to an end.

I continued to look for any possible way to reverse the decision to close the centers. I knew there would be a continued and ongoing demand from around the country for our services. Future trends seemed to indicate that with the emergence of technology, the laying off of professional and executive employees was only going to continue to grow. I knew that no one could do it better, and that we needed to help these employees who were losing their jobs in masses.

When it seemed like all doors were closing on continuing to help the growing number of people on the street without jobs, or the know-how to secure another one, I filed a DBA, named my company Career Visions Inc., and ventured out - helping companies and their employees find new jobs and new ways to make a living.

It has never felt like work to me, rather it always felt like what I was meant to do in the world. It is my calling or Ministry.

Without knowing how, somehow, I was miraculously guided and directed to help these companies transition and transform their work-forces. What I found was that starting at the executive levels, leaders and managers feared laying off employees. Particularly in the early days, when employees had never been laid off.

From the naming of my company Career Visions Inc., to the programs I designed, some-how, I had a natural knowing that employees losing their jobs had to let go of their old their job titles, and the sense of identity attached to them, when they were released from their jobs. I began to stay up at night and design programs after my two small children went to bed.

The first program was training and educating executive teams, HR and managers on how they should release the individuals – with dignity and respect. The employees had been with these companies for years and had the expectation that they would retire with the company. In many cases, the executive team and manag-ers were in shock and denial that they were having to lay off employees to survive. The business reason for handling these downsizings in a compassionate manner was for the internal and external PR and reputation of the company.

One of the biggest reasons for handling the layoff in a compassionate manner was not only for the departing employees, it was for the surviving employees. Being laid off affects the entire family, finances, and most importantly physical and emotional well-being. If I could get into a meeting with a manager before they laid off the employee, and coach them to deal with the message without fear and help them to eliminate their perceptions and their own survivor guilt in a thoughtful and compassionate manner, it set the tone for our subsequent work with the remaining employees who also suffered major losses. The loss of their colleagues, the restructuring of their previous workload, and the constant fear that they could be next.

The day after a major layoff, our career centers were generally filled with people in shock and paralyzed by fear. The majority had not slept the night before. They were usually trying to figure out what they did wrong, blaming someone for their fate, and playing worse-case scenario in their minds. An example of worse-case scenario is that they are leaving a company with a year or more's severance and salary, and on the way to the career center they pass a homeless person on a corner and imagine they will be on a street corner in a few months.

Typically, they are focused on what they don't have. If they don't have a college degree, they focus on the impending doom of not having a college degree, even though they have years of valuable experience and are very talented and gifted. In those cases, I always pointed out some of the greatest revolutionaries of our times, Bill Gates, Michael Dell, Steve Jobs, Oprah Winfrey, Ellen DeGeneres and Rachel Rae - none have college degrees.

If they are over fifty, they blame their age. I counter that with pointing out that in the 2016 election, the three final candidates in contention for the highest office in our nation, President of the United States, were all close to seventy. What if the three of them had that mindset, and focused on the fact that the last President elected in the U.S. was much younger? What if they doubted and feared they couldn't do such a huge job because of their age? The three top contenders were competing in a field of some of the most highly skilled political leaders in our country, all younger. Rather than take on that mindset, each of them campaigned passionately, effortlessly and tirelessly for over a year - with the energy and zest of other candidates who were more than twenty years younger. Even though all three had different political convictions, what seemed to drive all of them was their love for our country and their inner conviction that they could make a difference.

The process for interviewing for a job is the same as a presidential election, but fortunately not as cut-throat and vicious. There are generally three to five final candidates for any job, and it is not the most skilled job seeker who usually gets the job. It is the one who can convey and communicate with confidence and conviction why they are the best for the job in the interview process. It is the individual who overcomes all fear, self-doubt and false limiting beliefs - the individual who believes in themselves.

The Law of Attraction says that you are a "living magnet" and that you invariably attract into your life the people, ideas, opportunities, and circumstances in harmony with your dominant thoughts. When you think positive, optimistic, loving and successful thoughts, you create the magnetism to attract the very things you are thinking about. If you can keep your mind clearly focused on what you want, and refrain from thinking about what you don't want, you will attract everything you need to achieve career success.

First, you must have a vision, then you must keep focused on your vision.

Awaken to the Career Vision Within

"The eye through which I see God is the same eye through which God sees me; my eye and God's eye are one eye, one seeing, one knowing, one love"

~ Meister Eckhart

Every great idea begins in the mind before it shows up in form. Before the first airplane was built there was a vision for it. Before the invention of the light bulb, the first cell phone, there was a vision for it. Having a vision is undoubtedly the blueprint for setting an intention to find a new job, starting a business, or any goal you want to achieve.

Two useful practices are visualization and visioning. There is a difference.

When I began to vision living a life, I loved living, I developed a Vision Board by clipping from magazines pictures that resonated with me and portrayed scenes of what I wanted to feel and experience in the future.

I visualized and focused on what I wanted in my life versus what I did not wish to attract, and it seemed like my life entered a state of flow.

When we get clear and can see, visualize and feel through visioning what we want instead of what we don't wish for, things seem to happen miraculously.

Visualization

Visualization is a process where you are controlling the vision or image. Visualization uses the power of the imagination. For example, you decide you want to purchase a new car. You first start surfing the internet looking at cars, colors, makes and models that resonate with you. Next, you take time off at lunch and start visiting car dealerships and looking at the car. Amazingly, you may find that if you like a specific vehicle, model and color, you will start seeing it over and over as you drive around - that exact car!

The same is true for visualizing your ideal job, next career or business. First, you want to see a picture of it clearly in your mind. What are you doing? Who are you working with? What does your office look like? Where is it located?

Visualization works from the outside-in. You begin with a clear and reliable picture of what you want, then through focusing on that image, you visualize what it would be like to have what you desire. Think about your process in buying your last house or car. Once you're able to visualize what you desire, you are able to internalize and then experience how you want it to feel.

Three years before I started my business, Career Visions Inc., I was working with companies, facilitating six-week life design seminars, which included a program to vision and attract. Subsequently, I began co-facilitating the seminar series with individuals and in corporations. Proverbs 29:18 says, "Where there is no vision, the people perish." Having a vision proved correct for me. In this seminar, I became intentional about how I wanted my life to unfold. Developing a life vision, life mission and life purpose statement was impactful, powerful and entirely changed my life.

It was in this seminar that I developed my first vision board. I was a teacher at the time, and the image of a very successful, high-powered woman in a business suit resonated with me. A large house in an upscale neighborhood, an airplane, a downtown skyline, and vacationing and relaxing on a beach in Hawaii also resonated with me. When I returned from my first seminar, I threw the vision board in the back of a hidden closet under the stairs where we stored our holiday decorations and never looked at it.

Four years later, while getting out my Christmas decorations, I stumbled across my vision board. I sat in astonishment; every picture I had put on the vision board had not only manifested in my life but was even more than I had imagined. My professional work attire was now a business suit as I was helping an impressive list of Fortune 500 companies reemploy their employees affected by significant restructurings. I now had two corner offices in high-rise buildings in Houston and one in New Orleans. I was in the process of opening three offices in the San Francisco Bay area, one a corner office on the 28th floor of a downtown high- rise building with two windows, one facing the Golden Gate Bridge, and one facing the Bay Bridge. I remember at night standing in my corner offices around the country looking out at the lights and pinching myself. I would ponder, think, and give thanks as I reflected on how different this was from my previous life of standing in the halls or a cafeteria of a high school and monitoring students.

Every couple of years, I sit down the week between Christmas and New Years with a poster board, magazines, scissors, and glue and construct a vision board. In a feeling of gratitude and joy, I will cut out pictures that resonate with me of things that I would like to experience, see and feel in the future. Rhonda Byrne, an Australian television writer and producer, best

known for her book The Secret, in her sequel
The Magic calls this board a "Magic Board," and
suggests you put it in a place you often see and
title the board with "THANK YOU, THANK YOU,
THANK YOU" in big bold letters across the top.
Amazingly, even now I will look at my vision
board and to my surprise, the pictures I have
posted always seem to manifest in my life.

Four or five years ago I was going through
some health challenges, after my husband, and
significant other, had both passed within four
years of each other. I was in the depths of
despair dealing with the emotions of my losses.
That year I had difficulty filling my vision board
with pictures of the future that I wanted to
create.

All I saw was a picture of women in radiant health and a busy little toddler boy. Sure
enough, I now have that busy little boy in my
life, my grandson Ryder, and I now have the
energy, vitality and perfect health that I had in
my twenties. I also have an actual picture of me
propelling a waterfall last year on an eight-hour
extreme adventure in Puerto Vallarta, and it
looks almost identical to the image on my vision/
magic board of women in radiant health.

When helping others to construct their vision
boards, I caution them not to put anything on
the vision board they do not want to have appear

in their lives. On my first vision board, I placed a picture of the women in the business suit and she also had eyeglasses. The woman in the business suit happened, and so did the reading glasses. My 20/20 eyesight declined, and before LASIK eye surgery, I was wearing reading glasses. I tend to be a visual person, I see things in pictures. Some of my clients tend to be more auditory, they learn through hearing. I recommend writing out your vision, desires and intentions for the next two years, one year and six months. After you have completed your vision in writing, I suggest either recording and listening to your vision or looking in a mirror and reading it to yourself.

The late Richard Nelson Bolles, career expert and New York Times bestselling author of the job-hunting book What Color is Your Parachute, provides several exercises and keys to cut down the territory and be clear about what you like doing.

In his supplement, A New Quick Job-Hunting Map: How to Create a Picture of Your Ideal Job or Next Career, several exercises help you to prioritize and get clear on what you like to do with people, information and things. This helps you to define your favorite functional skills and evaluate how they are transferable to other industries, companies, or how they might be used in starting your own consulting practice or business.

Next, it helps to develop a vision of the physical setting you see yourself belonging in and feeling connected to.

- Where are the geographic locations you would like to work?
- Who are the people you like to work with and what are their qualities?
- Who are the managers you have enjoyed working for and what are their management styles? What is the spiritual or emotional setting that fits with your values and philosophy of life? What outcomes do you want to produce in the short term? The long term?
- What salary range do you want/need?

Chapter 8

VISION

"Your vision will become clear only when you can look into your own heart. Who looks outside dreams; who looks inside awakes".

~ Carl Jung

Visioning, on the other hand, is a different process. It is the process of working from the inside- out, using your internal power of intuition. Instead of having a picture in mind of what you want to see in your life, you get internally still so that you can see the vision as it comes to you. The visioning process allows you to open up to a higher idea for your life.

A powerful practice developed by Michael Bernard Beckwith, author of Life Visioning, helps you to develop a grander vision than you have imagined. You will come to see the best path forward in your work and life, it is a transformational adventure!

How do you go about this process?

First, find a quiet place where you are uninterrupted for about fifteen minutes. Perhaps play some spa or meditative music.

Next, if it is comfortable for you, close your eyes and take some deep breaths. Continue to focus on your natural breath as you practice this silence for five minutes. This process relaxes the mind and helps clear the mind from self-imposed visualizations/thoughts/ideas.

Begin to ask open-ended questions such as:

- What do I need to be shown to make my next move? What seeks to emerge through and as my career? My life? What is the highest vision for my life?
- What must I BECOME to manifest this vision for my career? What must I LET GO OF to manifest this vision?
- What talents, gifts, skills, and qualities do I already possess that will serve this vision? What do I need to know right now?

No matter how complete or incomplete, trust that more will be revealed. Say YES to this vision and know the highest and best for yourself.

- Enter a state of gratitude that this vision is emerging and seeking full expression. Open your eyes, wiggle your fingers and toes, stretch.
- Write down what you saw in your vision process, describe in detail any words, feelings, and actions that came to you.

I highly recommend the book Life Visioning by Michael Bernard Beckwith for further information and instruction on using this powerful process of transformation.

Chapter 9

DISCOVER YOUR LIFE PURPOSE

*"The two most important days in your
life are the day you are born and
the day you find out why."*

~ Mark Twain

C ircumstances and situations which seemed adverse at the time are what inspired and motivated me to make a big leap or career pivot from education into business. I knew it was time to recreate my life, figure out what I wanted to do, devise a plan and go for it.

Participating in the Education for Living Seminars, I began to awaken to new possibilities and opportunities in all areas of my life. The seminar company eventually changed its name to Life Design Seminars and started doing work in corporations. I began to enjoy assisting in the corporate division and eventually was hired to facilitate some of the six-week courses helping employees to design not only their work lives, their entire lives.

In the seminar, I realized that my life purpose or personal mission was to motivate and encourage others to discover their life's purpose and help them claim their maximum potential. I knew that I was here to add value to others and make a difference. At the time, this seemed elusive to me. I had no clue what job title or job description would allow me to accomplish this. My "why" or life purpose was to motivate and encourage others to discover their life purpose or calling and claim their maximum potential. I had no idea what the job title was or how to do that.

Do you have a personal mission statement? It is your internal compass for obtaining fulfillment, meaning, purpose and ultimately compensation while becoming and doing what you are called to do during your life.

Personal Mission Statement

A personal mission statement or personal philosophy summarizes in one or two sentences your why, what YOU feel you are to become and to do during your life. There are no right or wrong answers. Now is a time to vision, visualize, and reflect on your life and unique purpose or "calling" as you bring it into words.

Many people have never really thought about their WHY, their unique purpose or personal mission statement. If you have not considered your WHY, putting words to paper and contemplating on it for a few days will help you to develop your mission statement.

Although people write mission statements in many ways, the questions below may help you put the puzzle pieces together.

Name three people who have influenced your life:

1. What qualities do you most admire in each person? Are there any characteristics that are the same? Which do you want in your life?
2. What do you value?

3. Take this free assessment: Work Values Test. https://www.123test.com/jung-personality-test

Values Inventory

Once you have completed the assessment, circle your three top values from the list below. These are really important for you. After you circle your top three, read the definition of each and write the definition on the lines below. Spend some time thinking about how it would feel if you had a job or business where these needs were met.

Autonomy
Financial Reward
Work-life Balance
Working
Conditions Work
Relationships
Performance
Altruism
Creativity
Variety
Self-Development
Structure
Security
Influence

4. What do you want to contribute to your family, organization, community and or world?

5. List your key accomplishments or contributions that you have made or want to make in your life. Circle key words that resonate with you.

6. What things, people, situations or conditions do you want to have in your life?

7. Picture your 90th birthday party. In the table below, identify your most important roles in life and one key person that you interact with in this role. What would you want each person say about you?

	Role	Key Person	Statement
1.			
2.			
3.			

8. Now combine what you have learned about your most robust priorities and deepest values and develop your Personal Mission Statement.

I, (Name) believe that my "why," life purpose or personal mission is:

Chapter 10

KNOW THYSELF

*"Today you are you, that is truer than True.
There is no one alive that is youer than you."*

~ Dr. Seuss

Interests

Interests are activities that energize you most and fuel the passion in your career.

There are several ways to determine what you like to do. Go back through your career history and make a timeline of all of your jobs from the time you started working, as far back as to a child or teenager.

1. What were you doing?
2. What did you like doing?
3. What did you not like doing?
4. Describe a perfect day, what were you doing? What were you experiencing? How were you feeling?

My Next Move

An interest assessment that I suggest to anyone from high school through retirement is My Next Move. The Department of Labor offers this free interest inventory online. It ties into the dictionary of occupational titles and provides explanations of job titles, functions, salary information, and retraining and education resources. One of the unique features is there is a bright sunshine behind jobs that are in future demand. It also ties into data bases of posted job leads.

My Next Move is an easy-to-use electronic tool that enables you to explore what you like to do and helps identify your transferable skills. This streamlined interest assessment takes less than ten minutes and consists of only sixty questions. You can explore occupations and find related information including job openings, job outlook information, average national and local salary information, apprenticeships, and other relevant education and training programs.

In this integrative session, we will explore how to use My Next Move to decide and commit, to determine industries and alternative occupations to transfer your skills, to develop resumes using keywords for specific professions, and to develop and expand your marketing plan.

You can access My Next Move at: https://www.mynextmove.org/explore/ip

Once you have the themes from My Next Move, refer to your top three interests. The following information will help you to describe yourself in your career search. It will also help you to understand what motivates you, what you enjoy doing most, what you value and environments that are best for you.

Taking a battery of career assessments is very helpful in deciding what you want to do next and determining what companies hire people with your skills and interests. They are also beneficial in helping you determine if you are a good fit for a company based on your personality traits, preferences, and values. There are many assessments available, some are even free, but it is well worth the expense of hiring a certified career coach to help you better understand these assessments and develop career clarity.

My preferred tool of choice in working with people in Career Transition is the Birkman Method. The Birkman not only prioritizes your interests, but also measures your strength behavior - the behavior that works best for you or your most effective way of operating. Most importantly, the Birkman outlines your needs, or expectations and preferences you have, for the people you work with and the environment you work best in.

Understanding whom you want to work with, and the corporate climate that would best support you, is especially important if you've worked for the same company for a long time. The Birkman helps by predicting possible stress behaviors, which is extremely important to recognize during this process. Unmet needs can produce stress behavior, on top of which, most people in career transition are already operating in stress behavior.

In addition to providing the awareness of our actions under stress, the Birkman has an excellent Career Management Plus report that describes interests, preferences, preferred functions, operating styles and ideal work environments. Knowing this is beneficial, especially for people who have swum in the same fishbowl for years and suddenly find themselves overwhelmed as they explore new work opportunities. Additionally, there are also Birkman reports which provide advice on job search strategies, effective interviewing, and life and work balance in general.

Strengths

One of my favorite books is Now Discover Your Strengths by Marcus Buchanan and Donald O. Clifton. Based on Gallup research, the study makes a case for why each of us should strive to be working from our strengths versus attempting to learn how to do our weaknesses, or what we have no interest in doing.

After Career Visions won an award that gained media attention, a high-profile top-rated divorce attorney contacted me. I had no idea why he wanted to meet with me. After meeting with him for five minutes, the reason for our meeting became apparent. He wanted to discuss his dissatisfaction with his business and career. Despite his tremendous success and high income, he was dissatisfied with his job, running his practice, and his life in general. He joked that when he was working with people, they seemed to reconcile their marriages and did not get divorced, so he didn't get paid.

In coaching and training I watch people closely, they are like light bulbs. I call this lights on/lights off. When this attorney talked about his law practice, it was as though the light bulb went off. When he spoke about how he helped couples reconcile their marriages, the light bulb went on again. His energy and cadence would entirely change.

He hired me to do a battery of career assessments. When I asked him why he became an attorney, he responded that his father was an attorney and encouraged him to do the same. Based on the results of his Birkman, Strength Finders and My Next Move he had no interest in being an attorney, nor did he have the personality. He was a very empathetic, heart-centered counselor. He went on to become a marriage counselor and started to speak and lead marriage enhancement retreats around the country. He had found his calling.

Like the divorce attorney, I kept second guessing myself when I left the security of my $57,000 job as an administrator and teacher. There was perceived security for me in having a career with a teacher's retirement plan and health insurance, like my father. It was what I knew.

When I jumped off the deep end and started my company, I had no idea that within three years I would be making fifteen times my base salary, only now I had a 401-K (employer sponsored retirement plan) as well as health insurance that I set up for my staff and me.

I had no idea that within five years I could sell my company for several million. The title to Marsha Sinetar's book, Do What You Love and the Money Will Follow has indeed been my experience once I let go of playing small and discovering my calling.

Money was not my essential motivator. Instead, I was doing what I loved, and the money was following. The key benefits for me were the feelings of aliveness, fulfillment, joy, connections, and opportunities to meet and help some of the most gifted, talented and inspiring individuals around the globe.

When I received several awards for my calling to entrepreneurship to help people discover their purpose in life and claim their maximum potential, I was invited to speak and teach in boardrooms and at conferences with some of the most brilliant and inspiring corporate and political leaders of our time. I would never have thought this was possible when I took the big leap from my salaried position with a secure retirement. I could never have imagined that the newspaper would report "Career Entrepreneur Brings Vision into Action" when I was named the Small Businessperson of the Year.

We stay in work situations that make us miserable. Either the environment is not a right fit, or we have outgrown our jobs. I call this

Divine Discontent. The percentage of Americans on antidepressants has nearly doubled from 1999-2017. Researchers have found that one in six Americans, or 16.7% of 242 million, now take antidepressants. Moreover, most people who take them are doing so long-term. Rapid, accelerated change is causing us to operate under stress.

Fifty-four percent of Americans will go to work, stand around the water cooler and complain about their jobs. With social media, you only have to look at your Facebook page or see what people are saying on their Twitter accounts to know that they are settling for jobs that don't light them up. These employees operate in a victim mentality because they are either unhappily employed or underemployed.

The rise of artificial intelligence and other sources of work automation have sparked concern. Every day we read of corporate giants in trouble and laying off employees by the thousands because of rapid, unprecedented change. Online buying is replacing an entire retail store, technology and artificial intelligence are replacing workers. A recent Forbes article reported that by 2020, 50% of the workforce would be freelancers. This trend is not likely to reverse. Is this a negative trend? It will be for those who still cling to the idea of applying online for a job and waiting for some corporate giant to hire them. We watched our parents move out of an industrial age workforce to a workforce based on information. Rapidly, we are moving into a gig economy, which sees more and more employment being offered on a contract or temporary basis, rather than ongoing employment. These changes are requiring us to retrain and reskill to meet the demands of the evolving job market.

Think of Yourself as a Product When Looking for a New Job

What is your brand?

What are your strengths?

What makes you different from everyone else looking for the same function in the same industry?

You are as unique as your fingerprint, or as a snowflake under a microscope. I believe we are all here on earth to fulfill our life's purpose. You are on this earth, at this time, to shine your Light and express yourself as the Unique Emanation of the Divine.

Most people don't know what makes them different, what makes them unique. I was speaking at a job club and a young, intelligent, beautiful young marketing professional approached me in a shy manner. She was patient and very respectful and waited for everyone else in line to talk to me. She asked if I would help her. I agreed to meet her for thirty minutes at a coffee shop.

"I have a problem, it is my language skills," was her first statement.

She lit up when I said to her, "You have no problem, this is one of your key strengths as you speak five languages." I went on to explain that most Americans, myself included, speak one language, maybe two proficiently.

Our greatest natural strengths or differentiators are often our blind spots. We do them so effortlessly and readily we believe everyone can do it. Based on a Gallup study of over two million people who have excelled in their careers, the book Now Discover Your Strengths helps individuals discover their unique talents and strengths. The product of a twenty-five year, multi-million -dollar effort, the Strength Finder program introduces thirty-four strengths or "themes" and reveals how they translate into personal and career success.

Once you compile all the data from a review of your career history, your assessments and inventories, the visual illustration below shows the intersection of three circles, your skills, interests, and values. Peak passion, productivity, and a sense of aliveness happens when you get as close as you can to the intersection of these three circles. You are doing what you love to do, know how to do it and even do it well, and you are aware of your values. As you begin to explore new opportunities, it is essential that your values be in alignment with collaborators and organizations. It is here where passion, productivity, and profitability occur.

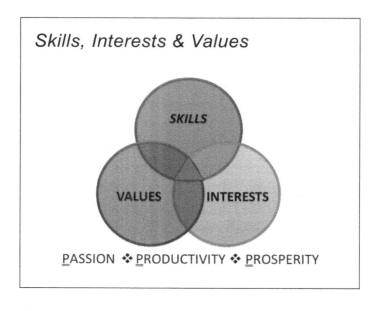

I know first-hand what it is like to work in a situation where the intersection of the three circles, skills, interests, and values was not even on the chart, let alone intersecting. My second husband was a veterinarian. My mother did not like animals, so we never had animals growing up, and I had never owned an animal. When my husband and I started dating, I would pull up in my business suit and staccato heals and call into the clinic and ask the staff to tell him that I was outside waiting for lunch. I didn't particularly like the smell of the clinic, the pet hair, or especially the thought of some big dog coming up and licking me.

When my late husband had a stroke four years after we were married, I began running his business. I thought it would be easy as it was one location and a tenth of the size of my corporation. I was very arrogant and very wrong. I had won high prestige awards like Small Business Person of the Year and Entrepreneur of the Year and prided myself on my entrepreneurial accomplishments. I thought I knew everything about running his business and that this should be a cake walk. I soon discovered this was not the case and learned many lessons.

First of all, my husband was an excellent veterinarian and surgeon, and had no interest and had paid no attention to detail or business operations for years. The systems and procedures were a mess for someone like me who needs things orderly and structured. Although I had managed hundreds of employees over the years in education and my professional services firm, my management experience was limited to overseeing professionals with advanced degrees who required little or no supervision. I was now dealing with a retail business, hourly employees who lived from pay check to pay check, a cash box, and controlled substances, all in one location.

My computer skills were marginal as a result of always relying on an efficient and effective administrative assistant. I had a total lack of education or understanding of veterinarian medicine, further compounding the situation.

I remember one particular Monday, several of the staff had called in sick, a typical Monday morning there, leaving me to greet a woman who entered the clinic with her poodle. As I nervously attempted to enter the information into the computer, I absent-mindedly asked her, "What is the breed of your animal, canine or feline?"

She looked startled as she reluctantly replied, "canine."

As I asked the breed, I could see she was considering running out of the clinic. In a shaky voice she responded, "poodle."

"Oh, of course, this is a cute little poodle," I replied.

My lack of interest, skill or knowledge hurt the business more than it helped. I felt exhausted, wiped out and frustrated after a few hours working there. It was a completely wrong fit for me. When we are working in our right function, in the right environment, we have the most excellent opportunity to express our Divinity and serve. I equate this to planting a fruit tree. You can plant it on one side of the house, and it will grow sturdy and bear fruit. You can plant it on the other side of the house, and it will wilt and die. What is the difference? The soil, sun and the amount of water all make a difference.

It's the same as doing what you love to do and working in an environment that you enjoy working in. Selecting the right culture is paramount. There are cultures like the soil where you will thrive, grow and feel truly alive, and others where you will wilt and die. Today's buzzword for this is "cultural fit." While I was not a cultural fit for the veterinarian clinic, I did end up loving the employees and doing what I do best, coaching them to discover their life purposes. The intersection of the three circles below will show where your peak passion, productivity and prosperity occurs.

Chapter 11

RESKILLING

*"The people who develop the
ability to continuously acquire new and
better forms of knowledge that they can apply
to their work and to their lives will be the
movers and shakers in our society
for the indefinite future".*

~ Brian Tracy

The slide below shows the correlations between your interests and skills.

When I am counseling individuals, the top row is not usually what derails a person's career. Because you have no interest, you have not developed skills in that area. As a result, companies will not hire you to do that particular

FINDING YOUR ZONE

function. If they do, it is likely to be short lived, like my experience at the veterinarian clinic. I have seen this happen, and it is usually in small mom and pop shops where they hire a relative or close friend. Fortunately, it is often a shorted lived career assignment. Unfortunately, it can ruin many a good friendship or cause heartache and upset in a family.

The next row, interest/no skill, is a developmental or learning opportunity. It is something the individual has an interest in and is willing to learn. These are growth or educational opportunities that will enhance the individual's effectiveness in whatever they desire to do.

When I left teaching and went into business, I had an interest, but had no skill or experience in running a business. I was young, and I had a lot of passion and energy. I was also foolish regarding running a business. Fortunately, my first employees were all former business executives with years of experience and initially ran the company, but they also taught me how to run it.

I also took classes to understand the fundamentals, like how to read an income statement, balance sheet, and how to better hire and manage people. I then went on to get a more formalized business education. I applied to MIT's Sloan School of Business' three-year Young Entrepreneurial Leadership Program. Selected as one of sixty from over 2000 applicants who had started their businesses before age thirty-five and had $5M+ in sales, this education was invaluable. I was one of five women selected. By the end, forty-two of us graduated from the program, and I was one of only two women.

Not only did I learn from some of the top business professors in the world, I learned from my exceptional peers. Motivational speaker Jim Rohn famously said that we are the average of the five people we spend the most time with. Learning new skills is like working out daily to develop a lean and fit body. It takes practice, dedication, time and the right coaches and trainers. Writing this book is another example for me of having an interest and limited skill. I have written curriculum for training manuals, presentations, and seminars. I have never published a book. The process is no different than when I learned to run a business and manage people. Like anything we want to learn or even excel at, it takes focus, time, hard work and dedication. It also requires reskilling, coaching and training.

For the past couple of years, I have been reading, watching YouTubes, Ted Talks, listening to audibles, and even attending conferences with speakers and authors I admire. One such speaker and author is John Maxwell. At last count, he has written over ninety-two books on leadership, business, and personal development and sold millions of copies. He is very intentional about adding value to people.

Books by Oprah's Super Soul writers and authors fill my shelves. I have traveled to many of their book signings, taken online classes and attended conferences just to be inspired and hear them speak. Now that I have started my book, I am taking classes, attending retreats, and I have hired coaches who know how to write, publish and market bestsellers.

In today's rapidly changing economy it is essential to reskill and retrain for future opportunities. It is also necessary to study and surround yourself with experts in the professions and field you want to pursue. Find out what it took to make them successful. Whether you are, or you aspire to be, an App developer, social media manager, Uber driver, prominent data analyst/data scientist, sustainability manager, driverless car engineer, YouTube content creator, drone operator, cloud computing specialist, or you want to be a millennial generational expert, surround yourself with people who are pioneers and experts in these fields and learn from them. All of these jobs were created in the last ten years.

My experience in working with people is that the biggest roadblock to career success and fulfillment is the next row - skill/no interest. Employees stay stuck because it is in their comfort zone. They falsely believe there is security in doing what they know how to do, yet have no interest in and are bored doing it. Often, they have even been recognized and rewarded for doing it well.

A more considerable danger in today's rapidly changing workforce is that an employee has skills which are obsolete, with decreasing or no demand for the skillset. When Henry Ford came along with the automobile, people who shoed horses had to find another way to make a living. Reskilling has been necessary forever, it is just rapidly accelerating today with new and evolving technologies, AI and automation.

As Stephen Covey said, "We need to keep our saw sharpened."

The movie Hidden Figures portrays the most excellent examples of proactive career management, career development and reskilling. If you haven't seen it, it is the incredible and previously untold true story of three brilliant African American women, Katherine Johnson, Dorothy Vaughan and Mary Jackson. They worked at NASA and served as the brains behind one of the most significant operations in history, the launch of John Glenn into orbit.

Each of the three women achieved career fulfillment in different ways. Katherine was a mathematical child prodigy and pure genius. With dedication and determination, she stayed focused and used her gift to calculate complex equations manually. John Glenn put his faith in her over the mainframe computer when it was time to launch.

Mary recognized the need for further education to advance in her career. With perseverance and persistence, she convinced a judge to allow an African American woman to attend school and obtain an engineering degree.

Dorothy managed a team of women who manually calculated numbers. Using vision and focus she could see that the mainframe computer would not only make her job obsolete, but it would also eliminate the duties of her entire team. Recognizing that there would be no need for her or her department to calculate numbers manually, Dorothy proactively and persistently found information on how to operate the mainframe computer and self-taught herself how to program it. She then went on to provide job security for the other women in the group by teaching them how to program the machines.

Think about it, the smartphone you carry around is millions of times more powerful than all of NASA's combined computing in the 1960's. According to the World Economic Forum's Human Capital Index, the pace of change is only going to get faster thanks to rapid advances in the fields of robotics, driverless transport, artificial intelligence, biotechnology, advanced materials and genomics. Jobs exist now that we had never heard of a decade ago. One estimate suggests that 65% of children entering primary school today will ultimately end up working in entirely new job types that aren't even on our radar yet. It is imperative that companies and employees follow the career management examples of Katherine, Dorothy, and Mary in Hidden Figures - forward thinking, reskilling, retraining and responding quickly to change and ever-changing technology.

When an individual has the interest and the skill, this is what I call the Zone. We are working in the flow. Katherine in Hidden Figures is an example of working in the flow or zone. Her inner genius is on display as she uses her Divine gift, skills, and talents with laser focus to compute numbers faster and more accurately than any man or mainframe computer. She exhibited this strength as a child and throughout college. She is a virtuoso, an individual who possesses outstanding technical ability in a particular field, whether it be music, art or athleticism. Her technical expertise is computing numbers.

A widow and single mom of three daughters, thanks to racist doctrine Katherine couldn't Even use a convenient restroom or coffee pot to get her work done. She continued to compute numbers whilst facing obstacles and adversity, such as having to run three-quarters of a mile, even when it rained, to use a woman's restroom that was permissible for African American women at the time. She could have been angry and bitter, hating the company and the people who treated her so disrespectfully. Instead, she stayed focused on her why, her life purpose, and as a result her contributions sent men into space.

I believe we are all virtuosos with unique strengths, gifts, skills, and talents that we are meant to share with the world. Beethoven, Michelangelo, Tom Brady, Oprah and Steve Jobs are also individuals who tapped into their inner genius, became masters and overcome any obstacle life threw at them.

Personal Values

What are personal values? They are the essence of who you are. Everyone is unique, we all have little differences that make us who we are. The process of discovering your personal values involves not just discovering what you are passionate about, but also finding out what is really important to you. The more we understand ourselves, the more self-aware we become, the easier it is to be successful.

In Chapter 9 the free online value assessment was recommended. If you haven't completed it, I recommend you do so now. https://www.123test.com/jung-personality-test.

Knowing what is most important to you will help you to attract the job, company or opportunity where you will thrive and feel happy and alive.

Chapter 12

PERSONAL BRAND STATEMENT

*"People don't buy what you do;
they buy why you do it."*

~ Simon Sinek

Once you have reflected on your mission, created your vision and reflected on your skills, interests, values, talents, and strengths, it is time to develop your personal branding statement. A personal branding statement is one to two sentences answering:

What you are best at?
Who do you serve?
What makes you unique?

It sums up your unique promise of value. It is not about you, it is about the problems you solve. Your personal branding statement is not just your self-identity, it is also your reputation and how others know you. A Forbes study asked individuals if how they defined their brand was how others felt and would describe them. 70% said yes. 15% were correct. Your brand is not about you - it is about your value. This study further showed that individuals whose self-identities matched the perception of others were more likely to lead more, win more and earn 10-25% more.

The best way to confirm that what you want to be known for is aligned with the image people have of you (and your personal brand) in the role, is to find friends or colleagues and ask them to be brutally honest.

Exercise

You can test your brand by doing the following:

List the five words that describe you (re-occurring words in career and personality assessments).

Ask five people who are close to you to state five words that best describe you. Now ask five people you don't know so well to say five words.

Asking for input will test your brand and help you to develop and modify your branding statement.

Who do you want to be defined as? How do you need to talk, walk, work?

How can you deepen relationships and build trust and loyalty?

What is your legacy, how do you want to be remembered after you are gone?

Personal Branding Template:

I help _____do_____ and solve _____ using skills that include _____

EXAMPLES:

"I help manufacturing organizations improve their processes to reduce waste and grow profits"

"I help thought leaders write great works in just 90 days"

Chapter 13

MARKETING PLAN

*"The aim of marketing is to make
selling superfluous."*

~ Peter Drucker

Once you have prioritized your interests and strengths and looked at what is most important to you, it is now time to develop a plan to find the companies or opportunities you would like to pursue.

A sound, well-constructed personal marketing plan is key to ensuring that you focus on priority actions and avoid wasting time on unproductive activities. As with any project, a good plan helps you organize and prioritize your work and keeps your productivity high.

Below are the four parts to creating a personal marketing plan.

Professional Objective with preferred functions. Positioning Statement with competency list.
Target Market, specifying:

a. Geographic location
b. Industry and type of organization
c. Size of organization
d. Organizational culture

Target List - List 30 – 50 companies that have positions and hires people for jobs you are seeking.

Fill in the Marketing Plan Template:

Date:	
Name:	
e-mail:	
Target Date to Land Next Job:	

Professional Objective:	

Positioning Statement:	

Core Competencies:	

Target Market	Geographic Area:	
	Types of Industries:	

	Size of Organizations:	
	Culture	

Target Companies:	

Chapter 14

DEVELOPING A RESUME AND LINKEDIN PROFILE

When someone loses their job, his or her immediate response is, "I need a resume, I need to update my Linked In profile!"

I have served on the executive management teams of two of the largest outplacement firms in the world. Their primary focus is to help candidates develop a job search skillset and immediately develop a highly professional resume and LinkedIn profile.

While well-written resumes and LinkedIn profiles are necessary for your job search, your resume is not always the best way to market yourself, yet many people believe sending out hundreds of resumes and attaching them to job postings on online sites will land them a job.

The Pros and Cons of a Resume

What is a resume? A short, professional account of your career, qualifications and accomplishments. The primary advantage of writing a resume is that it will help you organize your thinking and shows how your experience is proof of what you can do in the future. By organizing and defining your thoughts and accomplishments, it will help you express yourself more effectively during interviews.

Some people you meet will ask for a written introduction or summary of what you have done in the past, and it provides documentation for third parties acting on your behalf such as search firms or employment agencies. Occasionally, resumes open doors for you to build a network of contacts. It can be an excellent document to leave behind if it reinforces the impression you made in the interview. Someone may pass it around to people or companies who might be looking for someone with your qualifications.

More often than not, a resume can get in the way. It is a summary of the past and may not reflect what you want to do.

When You Respond to an Online Posting Consider This...

On average, 400 people will answer an online job opening. Generally, it will first go through software that scans your resume before it gets to the recruiter. It is not the most qualified candidate who gets to the recruiter, it is the person who can best match all the keywords in the job posting. This process is an arduous task that can take three or four hours of your time for one open position. In addition to being time-consuming, getting your resume to the recruiter is like winning the lottery.

Proceed with caution when passing out resumes, as it is not forward thinking, again it is historical by design. You want to talk about where you want to go next, versus where you have been. It can lead you back to what you have been doing, which may not be your goal. A resume can also be hard for your network to read and then think of a good job for you. Most people you know don't know much, if anything, about open positions, so sending them a resume may not help you.

LinkedIn Profile

LinkedIn is an essential tool. No matter if you are a current student or a high-flying executive, a professionally written LinkedIn profile can help open doors to opportunities and networks. Before LinkedIn existed, it was virtually impossible to connect directly with potential influencers, hiring managers, former colleagues or other individuals who share similar job titles to your own. With LinkedIn, not only can you create a future-focused online marketing profile, you can begin to connect to your network.

Creating a positive first impression is essential. When a hiring manager or recruiter reads your LinkedIn profile, they will typically make their opinion in twenty seconds. Having a professional, high-quality photograph is the first step. The old saying, "A picture says a thousand words." A Linked In profile with a picture is seven times more likely to be viewed. A professionally, well-written and completed profile that includes up-to-date information about skills and experience will help to get the reader's attention. Including key achievements, and examples of projects and value-added skills towards the top of the profile, will further maintain the reader's attention and create a positive first impression.

Build your profile so it is easy to find. To improve traffic to your profile, it is crucial to understand search engine optimization. Optimizing frequent visits to your profile is as important as the content. Having multiple titles and repeating them will increase your chances of your profile appearing in a hiring manager or recruiter's search. LinkedIn is a tool that you can use to help you network and get ahead in searching for new opportunities. Even if you are not actively seeking a unique opportunity, just having an account could change your career.

These are life skills that everyone needs, as the average job will last three to five years. While having both is essential and necessary to get another job, this is not the reason people stay unemployed, underemployed or stuck in jobs they dislike. Finding new opportunities requires taking action.

Chapter 15

ATTRACTING YOUR IDEAL JOB, NEXT CAREER OR BUSINESS

"Do you want to know who you are? Don't ask. Act! Action will delineate and define you."

~ Thomas Jefferson.

I f you are unemployed, the most effective way of finding another job is to approach your search like a full-time job, giving it at least thirty hours per week. According to the Department of Labor, the average job seeker spends five hours per week job searching. Five to ten hours may be appropriate if you are still employed and looking for another opportunity.

The Department of Labor also reports how jobs are found.

Internet 12 - 15%
Recruiters 13 - 15%
Networking 70 - 75%

People tend to spend most of their time on the internet and talking to recruiters versus networking to get to influencers and hiring managers. As Peter Drucker says, "Efficiency is doing things right, effectiveness is doing the right thing." Productivity and activity are not the same things. Sometimes we use action to deceive ourselves. Sometimes we need to feel busy in order to not have to do other essential tasks that make us feel uncomfortable.

I see this all the time working with individuals who are looking for new jobs. Finding another job or starting a business is a sales and marketing activity. If you are a CEO, CFO, engineer, IT, accounting and administrative professional, sales and marketing is probably not your top interest or something you like or have experience doing. Sales and marketing professionals sometimes have difficulty because the product they are selling is themselves. This is why focusing your job search on priority actions requires a targeted Marketing Plan.

Networking

Experts say that 70-80% of jobs are never posted publicly, which makes networking your way into those jobs a significant part of the job hunt. Typically, 60% of people find new opportunities by knowing someone. Traditional business networking is all about posturing and performing. Everyone asks the same tired questions, and everyone recites the same tired responses. We exchange business cards, and then nothing happens.

What happens when two or more people step out of the box and connect as individuals? Networking is about getting out and asking family, friends, former colleagues, bosses, competitors and industry leaders for help. It is about getting advice and connecting with people. Your goal in networking is to initiate and significantly enhance relationships. Through networking, you can get information on companies. You don't know whom other people know.

Ivan Meisner, CEO of Business Networking International, teaches the 12/12/12 approach to networking. The first 12, how do you appear from 12 feet away? First of all, people make decisions about you immediately, and you only have seven seconds. Do you look polished and put together, dressed appropriately and neatly for the occasion? With businesses operating so casually, my slogan is dress to impress. If you are looking for a six or seven figure salary, your image, energy and appearance needs to be a vibrational match for that salary. You can't look like you have been working on the house or changing the oil in the car.

Hire an image consultant if necessary. I also hear many senior-level professionals complain about age discrimination. I happen to believe it can be salary discrimination, more than age discrimination. However, this is where it is essential to update your image, improve your appearance and increase your vitality. In 2016, the three top Presidential contenders were all in or near their seventies. What if they had said, "Why should I run? Barack Obama was only forty-seven years old when he became President." They would never have run. The Pope is not young, and Mother Teresa was not young.

The second 12 in Ivan's 12/12/12 approach is how do you act 12 inches away? It is not just your appearance, what you say can be a real deal breaker. How is your attitude or EQ? How do you connect to the other person - with a smile, a handshake that impresses, good eye contact and confident tone of your voice? What do you say? Are you confident and upbeat?

Again, people hire people they like, people who have a similar energy to them.

Negativity, complaining and whining is a deal breaker. It not only lowers the vibrational energy and connection to the other person, but also reduces your vibrational energy. Change your thinking, and you will change your job search. Our brains are like master computers, every thought we think or word we speak is programmed into our minds. We attract what we are thinking. Positivity attracts positive outcomes, and negativity attracts negative results. The bible is full of talk about our thoughts, words and deeds. The 12/12/12 is for programming ourselves, as well as setting the impression outwardly for connecting to prospective opportunities.

The final 12 is the 12 words you use to describe yourself. Through introspection and career and leadership assessments, these 12 words succinctly describe "Who You Are"? This 12-word statement helps to avoid negative responses to uncomfortable questions. Avoid responses such as:

I am a "former" VP at Dell or IBM, laid off senior engineer from Exxon or Chevron. Worse yet, I was fired from Bank of America. The energy behind such statements is negative and doesn't invite further exploration.

How would you describe yourself in a positive way? I am a_____

Sometimes, job seekers will have two or three tracks they are exploring and pursuing. More importantly, it is about getting out and talking to people you know. In the initial stage, it is asking for advice on developing and refining a marketing plan. Executives may find this tougher because many rose to the top of their organizations and their self-sufficiency is a strength. They are typically decisive and make decisions fast, and patience is not their virtue. Now they are out asking for help and seeking advice, which is counter-intuitive to who they are.

Typically, in addition to high IQs, many executives have High EQs and reframing it as getting out and connecting to old friends and colleagues seems fun to them. Networking is a word that people fear. Oh no, I have to network. Networking is about building or reestablishing relationships.

My slogan is: Who should you network with? Anyone and everyone.

I was working with a young CFO of a major retail chain that was going out of business. His search had been going on for some time. He did not want to relocate and was seeking employment in the Houston area. One day while dropping off his child at his sister's on the way to a networking event, he spoke to his sister's next-door neighbor who was heading out the door to play in her woman's tennis club. He told the neighbor he was getting frustrated, funds were running low, and something needed to happen soon. She mentioned that she was about to play tennis with someone whose husband was president of an oilfield service company and asked if he thought that would help.

"Of course," was his reply, "at this point anything would help."

This individual not only had an interview within the next couple of weeks, but he also had a job.

People want to help you. I don't suggest you play the "I am down on my luck" victim story at networking organizations, with professional colleagues or hiring managers. However, friends and family are there to support, and some days it may be good to vent. The job search process is not natural, especially when funds are running low, and you feel like a star in the movie 27 Dresses - instead of always the bridesmaid never the bride, it can feel like always an interview and never a job.

What if Colonel Sanders had stopped at 1009 restaurants? What if he never called on the 1010th restaurant? He wouldn't be the Colonel today; he wouldn't have made billions and he would not have impacted the world. In addition to becoming a great businessman, Harland Sanders went on to become a philanthropist and donated his time and money to help people. My experience in watching people revision, reinvent and attract their ideal job, career or business follows the same path as Colonel Sanders. Once you know your chicken recipe, it requires dedicated effort and activities.

I heard a recognized recruiter and career coach ask this question to an audience.

What do all people who get hired have in common?

Participants responded with many answers. They have a great resume, they have a LinkedIn profile, a recruiter helped them, they posted online.

Maybe, but I have seen individuals get jobs with none of the above. The only thing every person who gets a new job have in common is that they skipped to the front of the line and talked to or interviewed with a hiring manager.

Chapter 16

INFORMATIONAL
INTERVIEWING

An informational interview is a scheduled meeting with an individual in a specific career or industry. It is important to remember that an informational interview is not a job interview and should be approached for the purpose of obtaining information.

There are several reasons why you should do information interviews. Some are listed below.

- Help you clarify your career goals and decide if the career you want to pursue is right for you.
- You will get an insider's perspective about opportunities at a company and knowledge of whether it is a good fit for you.

- Help you gain realistic information about a specific career, industry, or company.
- Your knowledge of the job market will expand, and you will hear about other career opportunities you might want to pursue.
- You will gain referrals to other professionals.

How do you get started?

- Start with people you already know – former co-workers, managers, customers, competitors, friends and relatives.
- Use the internet or LinkedIn to identify people in companies that hire people with your skills.
- Tap into your network to find people who work in specific companies or industries that are on your marketing plan.
- Call the company directly and ask for names of people who would be interested in talking to you.

What is the best way to contact people for informational interviews?

- Email, call, use LinkedIn or have someone you know contact the individual and ask if they will meet with you.

- Be sure to mention a mutual acquaintance if there is one.
- Explain that you would like to meet for 20-30 minutes to get their advice on your career search.

Sample – Informational Meeting Letter (no Resume)

Your Name
Phone E-Mail
Linked-In Address

Date
Addressee

Dear (NAME),

I am writing this letter to request a brief meeting.

I am a business professional with experience in (STATE FUNCTIONAL AREA).

I need the help of a professional like yourself to assess my management and business skills as they might apply to your industry currently, as well as to give me some direction on where my niche for growth opportunities may exist.

I cannot stress too strongly that this is not a disguised application for employment. I won't ask you for a position. Specifically, I'm seeking your insight into current industry conditions, as well as your assessment of my skills and experience in relation to current conditions. Of course, I'd be delighted to share anything I've learned during my professional networking activities, as well.

With the hope that we can meet, I will take the liberty of telephoning you (EARLY NEXT WEEK OR IN A FEW DAYS) to introduce myself more personally and arrange a brief meeting.

Sincerely,

Chapter 17

YOU ARE THE MESSAGE

New York Times bestselling author, Tim Sanders, states in his book The Likeability Factor, How to Boost Your L-Factor & Achieve Your Life's Dreams the following:

> "Likeability is more than important. It's more than practical, and it's more than appealing. Likeability may well be the deciding factor in every competition you'll ever enter. Job candidates are more successful if they're likable. They're more likely to get second interviews and more likely to get short-listed for jobs. They are also more likely to keep their jobs in bad times and in good."

Study after study shows that more often than not it is not the most intelligent, highly skilled applicant who gets the job. Generally, it is the one who was most likable, the candidate who went into the interview feeling confident, powerful, positive, engaging, warm and excited. Employers don't hire positions. Employers hire people with passion and drive who can fit into their company, and who they perceive will be great to work with and have the ability to do the job.

The interviewer has the following questions in his or her mind.

All the preparation that went into laying the foundation to your job search, knowing yourself, developing your personal branding statement, resume with quantified accomplishments and LinkedIn Profile have all prepared you to answer the first three questions:

1. Who Are You?
2. What problems can you solve?
3. Do you have the proof?
4. Can you help me and my business?
5. Will we like you? Will you be great to work with?

Preparing Your Mind and Body

"No beating yourself up. That's not allowed. Be patient with yourself. It took you years to form bad habits of thought that you no longer want. It will take a little time to form new and better ones. But I promise you this: Even a slight move in this direction will bring you some peace. The more effort you apply to it, the faster you'll find your bliss, but you'll experience rewards immediately."

~ Holly Mosier

Most people go to meet with a strategic connection, and especially an interview, feeling nervous and sweating bullets. Maybe you have prepared or even over prepared to know something about the person you are meeting with, the company, and formulated the right questions. Settling your mind and body immediately before the meeting or interview may be more critical.

Many people will frantically continue to prepare, review information, or slump over their cellphones answering emails and texts. These activities only intensify the anxiousness, nervousness, and lead to confused thinking. Rather than feeling powerful and confident, they enter a meeting or interview feeling powerless and fearful.

It is essential to arrive at a meeting place early and find a way to calm down and center yourself. If relaxing music, motivational messages or guided meditations resonate with you, listen on the road in the car. Be intentional about your thinking and the outcomes of the meeting or interview.

Visualize and reflect on the following:

- How do you want to feel in the conference or interview?
- How do you want the other person to feel?
- Focus on a positive outcome.

Getting the Job Interview

When an employer invites you to interview for a job, they already think you are qualified. Your resume, cover letter, job application and LinkedIn profile have already told them that you have the skills, education, and experience that they are seeking. If there is a phone interview, that is a pre-screen for these core skills before meeting you in person.

The job is yours to lose. The company needs someone with your skills, and the hiring process is taking valuable time away from their regular duties. Your challenge is not to change their minds. Employers want to like you as a person.

Question 4 and 5 above (can you help me and my business, will we like you, and will you be great to work with?) will require you to prepare both your mind and body for the situation.

Whether you are meeting someone in your network, a strategic connection, going on an interview or doing a pitch to bankers or venture capitalists, be prepared to answer these two questions. You can assume that there is probably more than one candidate competing for a position.

The differentiator will be your uniqueness, likeability, and ability to communicate that you can add value and solve their problems.

First, be prepared. And remember, you are meeting with another human being. Know something about the person. LinkedIn and Google are excellent research tools to understand the person's background and interests. Talking to people who know the individual can also give you insights into their personality, communication style, likes, and dislikes. People do not remember what you say, they remember how you make them feel.

Also, know something about their company. Spend an hour or more researching information on the company by visiting their website, and getting a company overview of the following information:

Company name.
Who is the company?
Its key differentiators from competitors.
Ideal clients.
Company culture.

In his book Good Leaders Ask Great Questions, leadership guru, author, speaker and coach, John C. Maxwell, discusses the importance of preparing in advance for a meeting with a person of influence. The same is equally true for job seekers – "good job seekers ask great questions." Preparing to ask great questions is as important as answering questions. It shows interest and that you are prepared.

Ask general questions: About the individual.
What is the work like? State of the industry. Skills and experience. Fitting in.
More information.

Chapter 18

DISCOVERING YOUR CAREER ZONE

"Start by doing what is necessary,
then what is possible, and suddenly
you are doing the impossible."

~ Francis of Assisi

Most of us have no trouble getting excited about the prospect of finding meaningful work, and it is a dream most people share. Purpose-driven work is not just possible. It is your birthright. The problem lies in the fact that many of us have come to believe that it is not possible, or is wishful thinking at best. In reality, nothing could be further from the truth. Like anything in life, with the right knowledge and tools, you can be empowered to accomplish anything you set your mind to.

In positive psychology, flow, also known as being in the zone, is the mental state of operation in which a person is performing an activity and fully immersed in a feeling of energized focus, full involvement, and enjoyment in the process of the activity. In essence, flow is characterized by complete absorption in what one does, and a resulting loss in one's sense of space or time. It is where you are present with what you are doing, and it's like the outside world disappears. Flow is where we feel focused, engaged, energized, connected and alive.

Named by Mihaly Csikszentmihayli in 1975, the concept has been widely referenced across a variety of fields, though the idea has existed for thousands of years by other names, especially in Eastern religions. Great athletes, musicians, inventors, successful entrepreneurs or business people have all found this state of flow or being in the zone.

I love to watch the Olympics. While the Olympics are going on for only sixteen days, we see first-hand athletes who have trained for their entire lives. A few young people, sometimes who we've never heard about, become household names and end up on the back of our cereal boxes. Why, because we get to live vicariously through these young, focused, connected, ener-gized and alive individuals who push their body, minds, and souls to their limits to achieve their goals. It is a natural state of consciousness that we all desire. For years, they have not only trained and mastered their physical bodies, but they have also trained their minds before they compete. They have prepared their minds and bodies to let go of any resistance and have a depth of awareness that is fully present, focused and mindful.

In an interview with CNBC, Mark Cuban describes his career success and journey to becoming a self-made billionaire, and how he uncovered that when using technology, he was concentrating so hard time seemed to disappear. In other words, he was doing activities where he was in the flow or zone. His career advice, "Rather than following your passion, follow your effort. Look at where you apply your time. You may not realize it yet, but how you use or don't use your time is going to be the best indication of where your future is going to take you. I was never into technology in college. I made one computer class and cheated on it, he recalls, but when I got one of my first jobs out of school using technology, it was like, wait, I love this.

I've taught myself the program. I could go seven hours, eight hours without taking a break thinking it was 10 minutes because I was concentrating so hard and so excited and loved it. So that's when I realized that I could be good at technology. Cuban went on to start a computer consulting service, MicroSolutions, which he sold to CompuServe in 1990 for $6 million. Five years later, Cuban and friend Todd Wagner created an online streaming audio service called Broadcast.com so they could listen to Hoosiers basketball games in Texas. Yahoo acquired the business in 1999 for $5.9 billion in stock.

Understanding what activities get you in your flow is essential. In an interview with CNBC, entrepreneur Mark Cuban attributed his career success to recognizing that when he used technology, he was so focused, so in the zone, that time seemed to disappear. A self-made billionaire, Cuban states on his blog that, "You may or may not realize it yet, but how you use or don't use your time is going to be the best indication of where your future is going to take you." From zero interest in school, to disappearing for hours at a time into technology in his first job, Cuban went on to be incredibly successful creating and selling technology-based businesses. He famously states, "Don't follow your passion, follow your effort."

Attracting Your Ideal Job, Next Career or Business Opportunity

We have all had times when things come together in an almost unbelievable, miraculous way. When events that were never predicted remarkably seem to guide us along our path. Carl Yung called this connecting principle synchronicity. In the beautiful flow of the moment, it feels as if hidden hands are helping us.

My quest to understand synchronicity arose out of a series of life challenges which pushed me into doing deep inner work which led to the process of spiritual transformation. Once I became clear on my life purpose and envisioned the type of life I wanted to live, it was as though the universe was conspiring for my good and propelling me into action. The right people and the right opportunities magically and miraculously seemed to appear in perfect synchronicity.

When my former husband's company was sold, the company provided a seminar for spouses of employees who could potentially lose their jobs. I went with a few of the wives. It was a great chance to get away for the night, go to dinner and attend this seminar. We planned to have a drink after the event.

The outplacement expert kept the audience in total victim mentality for over an hour as he continued to discuss all the potential losses associated with the impending layoff. I could feel my energy and the energy of the entire audience draining until finally, I could not take it anymore. I don't know what prompted me to do so, but I walked up to the front of the room, grabbed the facilitator's marker out of his hand, turned a page on his flip chart and said, "Ok, we have been talking about all of the losses for over an hour," I proceeded to draw a line down the flip chart, "now let's talk about the associated gains."

My husband was thirty-two years old and walking out of this company with a quarter of a million dollars. He made a lot of money for a man his age in those days, at $50-60,000 per annum. Also, he already had recruiters calling him, wondering when he could start with another company for more money. This is what society, 24/7 constant negative news, and some therapists do to program people to stay stuck in status quo and fear-based thinking.

Losing a job is right up there on the level of outside stressors with the death of a loved one or divorce. When an individual is told they are being laid off, because it means changing, most go immediately into worst-case-scenario thinking. Where am I going to get another job? How are we going to pay our house note? What if we have to live under a bridge? Keeping them focused on what they have lost and what they should fear versus what they have to gain in life and what is possible is not productive.

I helped the audience focus on the positive. Suddenly the energy shifted, and the room seemed to come alive again. When the presentation was over, some of the audience followed my friends and me across the street to have a drink. A few wanted my phone number to discuss their strategies for looking for jobs. On the ride home, my friends were quite puzzled and asked me how I knew how to offer career advice when I did not know anything about helping people find jobs. We all laughed.

All I could figure was that I was raised in a mining town where everyone was on strike and out of work every year or so. My family and the folks in my hometown seemed to know how to pick themselves up and move forward. Personal resiliency is the positive attribute attained by living in an immigrant family that had endured much adversity, yet always had faith and continually strived for a better life.

It was that night that I discovered my true gift and talent was to uplift people from the status quo to their highest potential. When some of the participants in the audience made known to the Outplacement Company the fact that I helped them, they called me to see if I would be interested in being one of their career coaches. They hired me, and within six months I was promoted to Assistant Director of their career transition and retraining program. We helped thousands of employees from several Houston-based companies, who were laid annually off due to corporate restructurings, mergers, acquisitions, and downsizings. The executive outplacement expert who facilitated the job loss seminar for spouses was working for me.

Developing a Job Search Mindset

A career coach or outplacement firm is excellent for providing a job search skillset which includes developing a resume, LinkedIn profile, and interviewing and negotiating skills. My perception is that the toughest part of a job search or starting a business is not just the messaging, it is having the presence, perseverance, resiliency, and faith to keep going despite all rejections and obstacles.

Helping an individual develop a job search mindset and let go of the baggage from old conditioning, habits, and beliefs from the past are the biggest hurdle. It is helping individuals to release their identities to former company and title. It is letting go of the embarrassment when someone asks, "What do you do?"

What I have observed in the thousands of unemployed people I have worked with is that pride gets in the way. I do an exercise to help them evaluate the losses. I have them look at why they are not getting out and talking to people. A response I get often is, "I am a failure." Really? A failure? They have held successful careers for years, achieved and overachieved to climb to the top, sometimes at the expense of other areas of their lives, and they feel like a failure because a company has merged, been acquired, reorganized, or their function has been made obsolete. Their self-confidence is often shattered.

If they have a spouse, it is essential to work with the spouse as well. Both are in transition.

Many times, the spouse is not used to seeing their go-getter husband or wife in a state of despair, discouragement or even situational depression. It is opposite to their usual operating style. Also, they have to renegotiate more time together as their structure and time together has changed. Helping them to see how valuable they are to their family and community is vital. Getting them out serving in volunteer activities that they enjoy helps to make them stay productive.

Getting past fears, reasons, doubts, and embarrassment helps them see that they may have lost their job, yet their strengths, skills, and talents are still intact and meant to serve the world.

Unfortunately, some never get past the loss of their past position and give up. Naively, individuals who have lost their jobs often search for work in the same way they looked for work when they were getting out of college. They do not recognize that the world of work has changed drastically. How often do we hear this syndrome with professional athletes who retire before age forty and sit in bars and reminisce about their careers and the specific game plays? On the flip side, we see professional athletes from the same team retire, recreate their lives, grow large businesses and transform their communities.

Positivity attracts positivity. Conversely, negativity attracts negativity. Amy Cuddy, an American social psychologist, author, and lecturer known for her research on stereotyping and discrimination, emotions, power and nonverbal behavior, summarizes how little power poses can make significant changes. Her core identity as a bright, intelligent student was taken away from her in an accident when her brain was injured and her IQ dropped two deviations. Overcoming this personal adversity, she says, "Rather than fake it till you make it, fake it till you become it."

Many individuals who lose their jobs also lose their core identity. Her research demonstrates how hormone levels change after people take two minutes in an elevator, bathroom or another private place before an interview, meeting or speech and do a "power pose." A "power pose" is an open and expanded pose. In her TED talks and YouTubes she summarizes her research, which shows, "Our bodies change our minds, moreover, our minds change our behavior, and our behavior changes our outcomes."

Chapter 19

DEVELOP A SUCCESS AND MONEY MINDSET

"There are no limitations to the mind except those we acknowledge. Both poverty and riches are the offspring of thought"

~ Napolean Hill

E arl Nightingale was a world leader in the personal development movement and author of one of the greatest motivational books of all times. First published as a spoken word record in 1957, The Strangest Secret defines success as the progressive realization of a worthy goal. Earl said, "If someone is working towards a predetermined goal or intention and knows where he or she are going a person is a success. If they are not doing that, they are a failure." He went on to say that we learn to read by the age of five or six, how to make a living by twenty-four or twenty- five, and by age sixty-five only 5% are financially independent. This statistic was accurate in the 1950's and is still true today. Why are we not financially independent? We confirm and act like the 95% who do not succeed. We believe circumstances or exterior conditions shape our lives. We are outer-directed versus inner-directed.

Those who achieve financial independence are inner-directed and deliberately pursuing a predetermined goal. It is summarized simply in Napoleon Hill's title to his book, Think and Grow Rich. Those who do not achieve financial inde- pendence haven't trained their minds to think and grow rich, rather, they have bought into the thinking of others. This is why it is important to evaluate our thoughts, beliefs, values, attitudes, habits, training and perceptions about success and money.

Our beliefs are a state of mind, and we often think something to be real without evidence that it is true. Our attitudes are the way we think and feel about someone or something. We have discussed and even assessed the importance of our values, again what is most important to you? Our thoughts, beliefs, attitudes, and values form our habits. We begin doing what we do for a reason. The pattern is programmed in our minds even though the idea may no longer be valid. We develop the practice through the training of others - our parents, teachers and social and cultural influences that tell us what is right. Today, with 24/7news and social media, we are programmed with constant negative news which may or may not be accurate. We develop perceptions by observing the external world and form conclusions without necessarily having full comprehension of the truth.

Transforming your perceptions about money, success, inner fulfillment, happiness and achieving your dreams requires that you examine your limiting beliefs and perceptions. It is essential to reframe these disempowering beliefs into empowering beliefs in order to form new habits and produce different results. Albert Einstein defined insanity as doing the same thing repeatedly yet expecting different results. You can't begin to do things differently until you are fully conscious of what is driving your habits and behaviors.

What are Your Thoughts, Beliefs, Attitudes, and Feelings Towards Money?

Complete these sentences:

Money is

Money means for me

Here are some of the most common limiting or false beliefs about money. Underline any of the ones below that you identify and add your own:

Money is the root of all evil.
It's only money.
The rich get richer, and the poor get poorer.
I am just not good at handling money.
Money doesn't grow on trees.
I come from a low-income family.
There is never enough money.
You have to work hard to get wealthy.
It is better to give than to receive.
It is selfish to want much money.
Other.

Without judgement, from who and where did you hear these false beliefs?

Look at your checking, savings, 401(K). This is the actual out-picturing of your past thinking, beliefs, feelings, and actions.

Now think about what you would like to have as your net worth. How will you feel when you have this amount? Write the amount you want to achieve and about how you will feel. Make sure what you write is future-focused, positive and affirmative.

This is your new belief or truth statement. Post this statement somewhere you will see it to help you remember. When you have trouble focusing, or believing your new truth statement, take out your wallet and coin purse. Look at every penny, nickel, dime and quarter in coins. Now look at every bill in your wallet, whether it is a dollar bill, five, ten, twenty, fifty or a hundred- dollar bill. What is the one thing written on every piece of money?

"In God We Trust." Our founding fathers knew the truth.

Most of us do not fully believe that we live in a universe that is for us, and filled with friendship, love, human interest, and helpfulness. Instead, we approach our career searches and lives as though it is a hostile environment out there, dog eat dog, and we have to drive and compete to get ahead.

The truth is that life is reciprocal. When we give of our passions, skills, Divine gifts and talents fully and freely we receive money, fulfillment, joy, and aliveness.

Chapter 20

NEGOTIATING SKILLSET

*"Ask, and you shall receive, seek, and
you will find, knock, and the door
will be open to you."*

~ Matthew 7:7-8

Negotiating

Now that you have attracted your dream
opportunity, it is time to expand your
negotiating mindset and skill set. Before
you start negotiating your ideal job, next career
or business, it is essential to examine your
thoughts, beliefs, attitudes, and feelings towards
money, success, inner fulfillment and achieving

your dreams. You don't get wealthy by just working hard. You get wealthy by creating real and lasting value for others and then offering it at a reasonable and fair price. This is true if you are employed, self-employed or a business owner.

First, what are the critical characteristics of a successful negotiator?

The first step is preparation and doing your homework. Begin by determining what your ideal salary number is. What are you willing to settle for? It is essential that you do market research. Talking to company insiders directly and asking questions of hiring managers is the best method. Remember, do not start negotiating before you have an offer.

Other characteristics of a successful negotiator include demonstrating a confident, calm and positive attitude throughout the process. It is helpful to continually mention how you can benefit the employer and add value. Remember, an employer is paying you to produce results. It is also important to be collaborative, flexible, and realistic in your demands. An employer is also looking for you to work well with the team. Be committed to a win-win outcome and be a good listener and ask great questions. Asking the right questions requires research and preparation.

How do you negotiate for a job you love doing, in an environment you enjoy working in, with the people you enjoy working with? Go back to your Values Inventory in Chapter 9 and look at the three values that were most important to you. While an offer will generally include the base salary and benefits, it is imperative to see what else is important to you.

You can use the internet. Below are some internet sites that can give you information about jobs in your geographical location:

- salary.com
- LinkedIn.com
- glassdoor.com
- salaryexpert.com/salarycalculator

Filling Out Applications or Ads

The first rule of negotiating is that the one who speaks first loses. That means you must handle salary questions throughout the job search process. How do you deal with salary question in applications or ads? Leave the information blank if possible. That is getting more difficult as the computer may not let you apply if this is blank. If possible, fill in "open" or "negotiable." If you know the employer's salary range for the position, state your requirement with the top of the employer's range as your midpoint. This question is a screening question. If you come in too high or low, you probably won't advance to the next step.

Screening Interview or Interview

The next step is usually an initial screening interview with a recruiter or the human resources department. It could also be an actual interview with a hiring manager. Again, don't forget the first rule of negotiating, the person who speaks first loses. Below are some possible responses.

Acknowledging an Offer

When you receive an offer follow the steps below:

1. Thank the employer.
2. Show your enthusiasm.
3. Clarify your position responsibilities and the results you expect.
4. Clarify your salary and benefits.
5. Request additional information if needed.
6. Express why the company and the job are appealing to you.
7. Ask for the offer in writing.
8. Ask for time to evaluate the offer.

DO NOT START NEGOTIATING AT THIS TIME.

Prepare for the Negotiating Discussion.

It is now time to prepare for the negotiating discussion. The main thing to consider when negotiating a salary offer is what is important to you in addition to the base salary and benefits. Now is the time to ask for what you want. Revisit your Values Inventory in Chapter 9 and look at your top values again.

Autonomy
Creativity
Variety
Self-Development
Structure
Security
Influence
Performance
Financial reward
Work-life balance
Working conditions
Work relationships
Altruism

Now compare the list below of options you want to consider in addition to the base salary and benefits.

Base Salary
Bonus
Incentive compensation
Commissions
Stock options
Profit sharing
401(K)
Retirement plan
Medical benefits
Insurance
Vacation
Equipment: car, phone, other
PC Salary increase timing /%
Tuition assistance
Job title
Work from home
Flexible work schedule
Other.

To prepare for the negotiation meeting, begin with the base salary. If it is different than what you were expecting, be truthful and ask if it is possible to get closer to your expectation. Other options might be asking for incentive or bonus compensation to supplement the base salary.

Maybe additional vacation time or other benefits may position the compensation package closer to your expectations. Finally, ask for a three or six-month salary review and suggest a percent.

Next, from your top values, compare it to the list of options to negotiate. For instance, if autonomy is important to you, maybe you ask to work from home a few days a week. If self- development is vital, inquire if tuition assistance is an option. If work-life balance is your top value, see if a flexible work schedule or additional vacation is possible. If performance is essential maybe you negotiate your title. It is easier to negotiate title for small to medium-sized companies.

Negotiating Discussion

Now you are prepared for a negotiating discussion in person or on the phone with the hiring manager. It is imperative that you tune in to the non-verbal communication and energy of the individual you are negotiating your package with. This is why it is best to avoid doing this via email or text. Follow the suggestions below for meeting to negotiate your next opportunity:

1. Tell the manager you have thoroughly considered the offer.

2. Express excitement about the opportunity.
3. Indicate that you have several areas for discussion.
4. Communicate the expectation that you both want a positive outcome and your belief that you can work through the areas for discussion successfully.
5. Indicate areas of agreement FIRST.
6. Discuss and resolve differences.
7. Affirm the agreement and accept the offer.
8. ASK FOR CONFIRMATION OF THE FINALIZED OFFER IN WRITING.
9. ESTABLISH YOUR START DATE.

Congratulations! Now is the time to celebrate and begin to prepare for your first ninety days.

Chapter 21

DESIGN A LIFE YOU LOVE LIVING

"Work like you don't need the money,
Love like you have never been hurt,
sing like no one is listening, Dance, Dance,
Dance Like no one is watching..."

We spend most of our adult waking hours working. Today more people want and expect their jobs to provide not just a paycheck but also human needs like life-long learning, community, fulfillment and a sense of purpose. Satisfaction at work is influenced by factors such as fair pay and benefits, work relationships, commute length, having a great boss, a clear career path, opportunities to learn, and working with a clear sense of purpose. A career adds to your happiness in life. Regardless of your circumstances, this boils down to living a well-rounded life. Maintaining your health and well-being, fostering loving, supportive relation-ships, having an experience outside of work and having the money to afford it empowers you to live your life to the fullest.

Below is a Life Design Wheel. Put your name in the inner circle. Evaluate your satisfaction in each life area on a scale of one (low) to ten (high). Place a dot on the number associated with your perceived satisfaction. Now, connect the dots. If this was a tire on your car, how would it be moving?

Next, look at three areas that you would like to act and set goals on from the next page. Finally, develop a Vision Board of your future desired state by clipping images from magazines.

LIFE DESIGN WHEEL

A Goal is Just a Dream With a Deadline

Wheel of Life categories identify specific steps that will move you from where you are today toward where you want to be.

Where you are now.	Where you desire to be.	What will you do to get there?	By When?
Career/ Livelihood		1. 2. 3.	
What is in the way of me achieving this and what do I plan to do about that?			
Family/ Friends		1. 2. 3.	
What is in the way of me achieving this and what do I plan to do about that?			
Intimate Relationship		1. 2. 3.	
What is in the way of me achieving this and what do I plan to do about that?			
Health & Fitness		1. 2. 3.	
What is in the way of me achieving this and what do I plan to do about that?			
Spiritual		1. 2. 3.	
What is in the way of me achieving this and what do I plan to do about that?			

Emotional Well-Being		1. 2. 3.	
What is in the way of me achieving this and what do I plan to do about that?			
Living Space		1. 2. 3.	
What is in the way of me achieving this and what do I plan to do about that?			
Play/ Self-Care		1. 2. 3.	
What is in the way of me achieving this and what do I plan to do about that?			
Financial Freedom		1. 2. 3.	
What is in the way of me achieving this and what do I plan to do about that?			
Personal Development Education		1. 2. 3.	
What is in the way of me achieving this and what do I plan to do about that?			

Never get so busy making a living that you forget to make a life!!! Choose to live a life with much joy, happiness, health aliveness, and prosperity. You deserve it. It is your birthright.

Last Page

Patti's training career began at the University of Houston, where she served as the Associate Director for the Center for Applied Technology. Her responsibilities included the development and delivery of technology and soft skills training to corporations throughout Texas as well as teaching and mentoring graduate students and interns in the Training and Development Department. Patti then envisioned and launched Career Visions, Inc., a Human Capital Firm specializing in Organizational and Career Change.

Career Visions grew to 31 offices nationwide in three years and earned recognition as the second-fastest growing privately held company in Houston. Her strategic leadership garnered her the Small Business Person of the Year Award from the SBA, Women Business Enterprise of the Year from the Houston Woman and Minority Business Council, 100 Best Companies in Houston to Work, and three consecutive nominations for Entrepreneur of the Year.

Lee Hecht Harrison acquired Career Visions, Inc. and Patti was retained as the Senior Vice President/Managing Director of the Gulf Coast Region. Next, she served as Senior Vice President of Global Sales, Services and Marketing for Right Management Consultants.

Over the course of her career, Patti has spoken and facilitated training for and consulted with organizations such as Chevron, Hewlett Packard, Exxon, Westinghouse, BP, American General Life Insurance, Wells Fargo, Dow Chemical, KSKJ Life Insurance, Memorial Healthcare System, McDonnell Douglas, Raytheon, NASA, Microsoft, Schlumberger, Core Staff, Halliburton, The Archdiocese of Chicago, Centers for Spiritual Living in Southern CA and TX, The Global Women's Forum, The International Women's Forum, National ASTD, SHRM, Women Helping Women, Orange County, United Way, Orange County, and Cal State Fullerton. She currently serves on the Board of Directors of Goodwill Central Texas and chairs the Strategic Workforce Development Committee and Austin Bridge Builders Alliance and serves on the steering committee for the Global Leadership Summit.

Patti holds an M.Ed. in Educational Counseling and Psychology and completed a three-year Executive Entrepreneurial Leadership program at the Sloan School of Business, MIT. She has

completed executive/leadership coaching cer-
tification programs with The John Maxwell
Group, Lee Hecht Harrison, Right Management
Consultants, Birkman International, Khorus,
DiSC Workplace, Management Research
Group, ProAdvisor Coach, MindScan, and New
Horizons – Retirement Success Profile and Life
Options Profile. She is a dual-licensed Spiritual
Practitioner with Agape International Spiritual
Center, Los Angeles, CA and the Center for
Spiritual Living, Golden, CO.

For more information regarding her Speaking,
Training, and Career Coaching Services, please
visit her website at www.purepotentialconsult-
ing.com.

REFERENCES

AZ Quotes. "Quotes. Author M. Michael Beckwith." Accessed September 9, 2018. https://www.azquotes.com/quote/667442

Beinkandescent. "Quotes. Holly Mosier." Accessed September 13, 2018. https://beinkandescent.com/articles?c=quotes

Blog Maverick. "The Mark Cuban Weblog." Accessed September 13, 2018. http://blogmaverick.com/2012/03/18/dont-follow-your-passion-follow-your-effort/

Bridges, William. Transitions: Making Sense of Life's Changes. 2nd Edition. Ingram Publisher Services: US, 2004.

Buchanan M and Donald O. Clifton. Now Discover Your Strengths. Free Press: New York, 2001.

Emerging Spirits Center. "Ernest Holmes on Prosperity." http://emergingspirits.org/2017/03/27/dr-larkinernest-holmes-on-prosperity/

Gallup. "State of the American Workplace."
Accessed September 9, 2018. https://
www.gallup.com/workplace/238085/
state-american-workplace-report-2017.aspx

Gallup. "The Engaged Workplace."
Accessed September 9, 2018. https://
www.gallup.com/services/190118/
engaged-workplace.aspx

Goodreads. "Simon Sinek. Quotes.
Quotable Quote." Accessed
September 12, 2018. https://www.
goodreads.com/quotes/668292-peopl
e-don-t-buy-what-you-do-they-buy- why-you

Goodreads. "Stephen R. Covey. Quotes."
Accessed September 12, 2018. https://
www.goodreads.com/author/quotes/1538.
Stephen_R_Covey

Goodreads. "Steve Jobs. Quotes. Quotable
Quote." Accessed September 9,
2018. https://www.goodreads.com/
quotes/772887-the-only-way-to-d
o-great-work-is-to-love

Goodreads. "William Bridges. Quotes." Accessed
September 15, 2018. https://www.
goodreads.com/author/quotes/5111924.
William_Bridges

Hendricks, G. The Big Leap. Conquer Your
Hidden Fear and Take Life to the Next Level.
Harper Collins: US, 2009.

Hill, Napoleon. Think and Grow Rich.
Revised Edition. Penguin Putnam Inc: Los
Angeles, 2007.

Kelly, Megyn. Settle for More. Harper Collins
Publishers Inc: US, 2016.

Marketing Insider Group. "Marketing IS
Business: The Wisdom of Peter Drucker."
Accessed September 12, 2018. https://
marketinginsidergroup.com/strategy/
marketing-is-business- the-wisdom-of-peter-
drucker/

Morrissey, Mary Manin. Building Your Field of
Dreams. Bantam, 1997.

Sanders, Tim. The Likeability Factor, How to
Boost Your L-Factor & Achieve Your Life's
Dreams. Three Rivers Press: NY, 2005.

Smart Recruiters. "'Whatever Your Life's Work
is, Do it Well,' said Dr. King." Accessed 1
September 2018. https://www.smartrecruiters.
com/blog/whatever-your-lifes-work-is-
do-it-well-said-dr-king/

Nightingale, Earl. The Strangest Secret.
(unabridged edition). Merchant Books:
US, 2013. YouTube. "University of Texas
at Austin 2014 Commencement Address -
Admiral William

H. McRaven." Accessed 1 September
2018. https://www.youtube.com/
watch?v=pxBQLFLei70

Made in USA - North Chelmsford, MA
1227129_9781641843638
01.21.2021 0834